Synaesthetics

Synaesthetics:

Art as Synaesthesia

Paul Gordon

BLOOMSBURY ACADEMIC
NEW YORK • LONDON • OXFORD • NEW DELHI • SYDNEY

BLOOMSBURY ACADEMIC
Bloomsbury Publishing Inc
1385 Broadway, New York, NY 10018, USA
50 Bedford Square, London, WC1B 3DP, UK

BLOOMSBURY, BLOOMSBURY ACADEMIC and the Diana logo are trademarks of Bloomsbury Publishing Plc

First published in the United States of America 2020

Cover design by Eleanor Rose
Cover image: Detail from "Red Moon," Monoprint, acrylic paint, cotton fabric, cotton thread © Andra Stanton

Library of Congress Cataloging-in-Publication Data

ISBN: HB: 978-1-5013-5679-7
ePDF: 978-1-5013-5681-0
eBook: 978-1-5013-5680-3

Typeset by Deanta Global Publishing Services, Chennai, India

Contents

Acknowledgments

Thanks to Haaris, Amy, and the wonderful staff at Bloomsbury with whom it is truly a joy to work.

I would like to dedicate this book to my wife Bridget, whose consistent interest in my work makes all things possible.

(*A Note on QR Codes*: I have chosen to use QR codes for the illustrations in this work. For those not familiar with how these work, just download a QR reader to your phone or laptop and hold it up to the code on the page and the image will appear. Thanks to Amazon Web Services (*AWS*) for their expert help in providing this technology.)

1

Introduction: Art as Synaesthesia

I may be wrong, but it seems to me that this idea [of a synaesthetic relationship between music and poetry] will stir the dreams of future generations.

(Debussy[1])

Art is everywhere, and has been so for a very long time. And yet, no one has satisfactorily explained the particular pleasure that is beauty, or the particular kind of meaning—truth, if you will—that is to be derived from that beauty except, of course, to famously refer them back to each other. Witness, for example, this statement by Hegel, which begins with the promise of explaining what beauty is only to end up acknowledging the impossibility of the same:

> If we are to display the necessity of our object, the beautiful in art, we should have to prove that art or beauty was a result of antecedents such as, when considered in their true conception, to lead us on with scientific necessity to the idea of fine art. But in as far as we begin with art, and propose to treat of the essence of its idea and of the realization of that idea, not of antecedents which go before it as demanded by its idea, so far art, as a peculiar scientific object, has, a presupposition which lies beyond our consideration. . . . Therefore it is not our present aim to demonstrate the idea of beauty from which we set out, that is, to derive it according to its necessity from the presupposition which are its antecedents in science. . . . For us, the idea of beauty and of art is a presupposition given in the system of philosophy.[2]

Following on the heels of a recent book that examined the attempts by Kant, Hegel, and other Idealists to define art in terms of the philosophical absolute or "thing-in-itself,"[3] the present work proposes a related theory of art as synaesthetic and, then, applies this idea to various works from various media, including works—such as movies, illustrated books, and song lyrics—that explicitly cross over into media involving the different senses. The idea of art as synaesthetic is not, however, limited to those "cross-over" works because, if my thesis is correct, even an individual poem or novel or painting calls upon different senses in creating its synaesthetic "meaning." This idea of replacing "aesthetic" with "synaesthetic" is a new argument that will, I hope, be made more convincing as one delves deeper into the synaesthetic unities discussed here as well as into the many more points of synaesthetic contact *not* discussed in this work; for example, that of dance as visual music; tactile, "textile art" such as that featured on the cover; architecture as having "a special role to play in the advancement of multi-sensory perception,"[4] and acting as the synaesthetic union between self and other.[5]

Although this is a new way of defining art, it has been anticipated by such things as Horace's famous *ut pictura poesis* dictum, discussions of the "sister arts" or *paragone* in the Renaissance, Baudelaire's (and the later Symbolists') occasional statements about poetry as synaesthesia and, more recently, by the field of "word/image studies" and its parent discipline of "comparative literature." However, such arguments have always been marginalized, often by the very artists and theoreticians who proffered them. With regard to Horace's notion, the idea of poetry as "like" painting (or vice versa) is not the same as saying that poetry *is* painting, and vice versa. Similarly, if the relatively new field of "word/image studies" has reached an impasse, it is because, I would argue, it is similarly deficient in not bringing together its two components where, in artworks, the word *is* image, and the image *is* word—*et verbum caro factum est.*

It is also important to distinguish "synaesthetics" from other ways the relation between art and synaesthesia has been defined in the past. As many have noted, interest in synaesthesia itself, as well as in its relation to the arts, has waxed and waned over time. A second renaissance, as it were, occurred in the nineteenth century, when the earlier obsession by da Vinci and others in the relation of the "sister arts," or *paragone*,[6] led some to argue even more strongly for the underlying unity of the arts: "the painter who is musical, the composer who paints, these are the true, genuine artists."[7] Curiously, the early nineteenth century was also the period when the idea of "absolute music" freed the medium from any ancillary relation to dance, theater, and so on.

It is precisely this "paradox"[8] of the simultaneous rise of "absolute music" with growing interest in synaesthetic forms like "program music," the Wagnerian *Gesamtkunstwerk*, Baudelairean *correspondances*, etc. that the "synaesthetic" model proposed here hopes to clarify, for the artistic "purity" advocated not only by advocates of "absolute music" but, with regard to the visual arts, by the likes of Lessing and, more recently, Clement Greenberg,[9] is based on a profound (albeit inevitable) misunderstanding of the very artworks that their conceptual categories seek to explain. As Schelling argued, all art is "absolute" (indeed, he even went so far as to claim that there is only One artwork![10]), and the result of this ontology is that the very "purity" of art sought by those who seek to define or sequester it is inherently syn-aesthetic, not aesthetic.

As Marsha Morton has noted in her excellent essay for *The Arts Entwined*,[11] two of the leading practitioners of the *Gesamtkunswerk* and "program" (versus "absolute") music, Wagner and Berlioz respectively, largely ignored painters and rarely visited museums, and while some might see this as contrary to their many examples of "visual music," I would strongly disagree, for it is based, again, on a profound misunderstanding of the nature of their art. If, as Morton also notes, other romantics such as Carlyle and Mme de Stael considered music, which had become the dominant art form of the nineteenth century, as "leading us to the edge of infinity,"[12] this "edge" combines the arts in a unified whole, whether or not the other arts are explicitly involved, as in opera, dance, program music, etc. or not. Indeed, it is more likely the case, for many of those (including Wagner[13]) who wrote against "program music," that the literal, as opposed to metaphorical, reference to this sort of sensory crossover actually undermines the very unity it purports to reclaim. There is nothing literally "pastoral" in Beethoven's 6th symphony, nor is the *Symphony Fantastique* literally about its hero's opium-induced fantasies; analogically speaking, such "tone poems" are to artistic synaesthesia as artistic synaesthesia is to synaesthesia proper.

So let the incessant arguing about visual/pictorial music versus nonvisual/pictorial music cease, arguing that has led some, for example, to claim that Corot's landscapes are more musical than, say, those of Monet.[14] The pseudoscientific claim to define art—"aesthetics"—as separate from its synaesthetic essence takes us further from our understanding of art because of the very act of understanding it this way. *Every artwork is a Gesamtkunstwerk*, for, as Edouard Schuré observed at the end of the nineteenth century, "Divine Art has been cut into pieces. . . . The arts constitute a united whole. They are truly fertile only when they act together in harmony and support each other."[15]

That said, to claim that art is inherently synaesthetic—that the aesthetic is really the "syn-aesthetic," beginning with the empathic unity between the spectator and the work—requires that one clarify at the outset the relation of literal synaesthesia, a widely recognized if still controversial neurological phenomenon in which one hears colors, sees sounds, tastes smells, etc. ("To persons endowed with coloured hearing, for example, speech and music are not only heard but are also a visual mélange of coloured shapes, movement and scintillation."[16]), to art *as* synaesthetic—what one writer refers to as the difference between "actual" and "artistic" synaesthesia,[17] and another as "psychological" and "cultural" synaesthesia,[18] and yet another as "developmental" versus "pseudosynaesthesia."[19] Although synaesthesia is often discussed in terms of the relatively few artists who explicitly define themselves as synaesthetes (Rimsky-Korsakov, Nabokov,[20] Messiaen, Hockney, and others) or the art*works* that explicitly define themselves as synaesthetic (this list is much longer, including works by Baudelaire, Rimbaud, Whistler, Klee, and others), no one has gone so far as to claim that all art is synaesthetic. With regard to this essential question regarding literal versus figurative synaesthesia, I will maintain that while there is clearly a difference between the neurological condition and its aesthetic counterpart, *the difference is one of degree rather than one of kind, and art owes its very existence to those neurological underpinnings.*[21] Although they seemingly reject the notion of art's relation to synaesthesia "proper," two leading experts in the scientific study of synaesthesia nonetheless pose the question:

> Given the varieties and degrees of synaesthesia that appear to exist, as well as the evidence for cross-modal transfer in normal people, an important question to address is: are people with synaesthesia qualitatively or simply quantitatively different?[22]

As the common metaphorical reference would suggest, "taste" (*goût, Geschmack*, etc.) is related to art, but it is not the same as eating it.

Resistance to this idea is bound to come from both sides, from writers on art as well as from synaesthetes themselves, and those interested in "real," "developmental" synaesthesia. The former would reject the idea as, at best, analogically true; that is, art might be *like* synaesthesia in providing many sensory crossovers, such as the all-important, ubiquitous presence of metaphor ("My luve is like a red, red rose"), but such a relation to synaesthesia, however important, must remain just that, a purely analogical relation. Synaesthetes proper, and those studying the neurological phenomenon, would similarly reject the idea because the experience is real and involuntary; the relation between a "trigger" (say, a number) and its "concurrent" (say, a color) is literal, not figurative. In a word: the thesis that art *is* synaesthetic must answer to the objection that art is, at best, *like* synaesthesia. As representative of both camps Dani Cavallaro mentions Jamie Ward (*The Frog Who Croaked Blue*), who insists that "most types of synaesthesia have little or no bearing on art."[23]

There are at least three preliminary answers to these important objections to the idea of art as synaesthetic, although these objections can only really be answered by the numerous concrete examples that make up the present work. The first, which is largely speculative but, according to Daria Martin's recent work on mirror-touch synaesthesia, has significant "scientific support,"[24] was first suggested to me by a scientist who has spent many years studying actual synaesthetes in his native country of Switzerland.[25] He believes that as infants everyone is originally synaesthetic, and that as we mature most of us progressively lose this inherent capacity. This would explain why art is synaesthetic while not synaesthesia as such—it is a "disinhibitor,"[26] a "remembrance of things past," a return to our earlier synaesthetic "consciousness" about which Proust would doubtless have had much to say. (This answer also fits well with Freud's theory of art as a window into our infantile Unconscious[27] and, especially, his notion of dreams as synaesthetic word/ images.[28]) It is also worth noting that if this relatively widespread notion of an original stage of synaesthetic "consciousness" is correct,[29] it is highly likely that it can, under certain circumstances and/or with a certain degree of practice, be regained in whole or in part. Of course, one would have to begin such "exercises" by acknowledging that our usual, abstract thinking about synaesthesia is, itself, hopelessly un-synaesthetic!

A second, related answer would argue that while there is clearly a difference between the neurological condition and its aesthetic counterpart, the difference is one of degree rather than one of kind, and that, as mentioned, art owes its very existence to those neurological underpinnings. This answer is supported by a recent and groundbreaking, albeit contested, discovery in neuroscience, that of mirror neuron systems:

> Mirror neurons are a special class of cells first discovered in the brains of macaque monkeys in 1992 by a group of neuroscientists in Parma, Italy (including Vittorio Gallese, contributor to this volume). The scientists found that single neurons in the monkey fired both when the animal performed an action (lifting a cup, tearing a piece of paper) and, equally, when it merely watched another monkey or person performing that same action.[30]

A third related answer would argue for a middle ground in which art *is* synaesthetic because it is *like* synaesthesia. That is to say, because no one has yet been able to define what art is (as noted at the outset, even Hegel, who wrote on art at great length, was forced to admit as much[31]), and because one has therefore only ever been able to say what art is *like*, then the fact that art is like synaesthesia means that, lacking any more literal definition, it *is* synaesthesia. The definition of art as synaesthesia is thus a catachresis, a figurative designation that is true because there is no literal designation to replace it. Moreover, this notion of art as synaesthesia is not just one figure among others but *the* figure of art, because it is a figure for the very notion of figurability—that is, metaphoricity— that is art, namely, the notion of replacing something literal with something other (cf. allegory, symbolism, mimesis, etc.). This notion of art as a valid "middle ground" between real and figurative synaesthesia would answer, I believe, the objection raised by Baron-Cohen and his scientific colleagues that art in general and metaphor in particular are "pseudosynaesthesia," an objection that has the unfortunate consequence of failing to account for the relation of art and metaphor to its obvious synaesthetic underpinnings.

Finally, one might also object to this view of art as synaesthetic by granting that while art may be related to our underlying synaesthetic tendencies, there is no use or value in approaching art this way because, as we admit, the experiences are very different. But, how different? It is this objection, and this question, that this treatise hopes to answer (or, at least, to begin answering) by examining concrete examples of various works of art from various media (poetry, painting, film, etc.) in order to demonstrate how a synaesthetic—versus merely aesthetic—approach serves to deepen our understanding of those particular works and, indeed, of art in general. Although art is not the same as "real" synaesthesia, that is because it is not the same as "real" anything. It is, however, the thesis of this book that art's relation to its synaesthetic underpinnings is essential to its creation, and that attending to its synaesthetic origins brings us closer to an answer to the question with which we began: "What is art?"

Synaesthesia as *"The Figure in the Carpet"*

The importance of Henry James' "little tale"[32] about the search for the meaning of art has not passed unnoticed by a number of influential critics (Todorov, Wolfgang Iser, J. Hillis Miller, and others), all of whom have offered insightful interpretations of this metastory in which readers of "The Figure in the Carpet" repeat the pursuit of the critics' pursuit of the "figure in the carpet" within the story, but none of whom have argued for it as having anything to do with synaesthesia. Like Iser's "reader-response" interpretation of the story,[33] I would like to use James' novella "In lieu of an Introduction" to my own "manifesto" on art as synaesthesia.

Even those who, like Iser, doubt the seriousness of James' story[34] cannot doubt the story's explicitly stated metatextual, and even "metaphysical," pursuit. For James' story, which might be seen as a harbinger of the revolutionary "New Criticism" that was to emerge some thirty years after James published the work, and only some twenty years after his important Preface to the New York Edition of this work, is explicitly about the right way to read literature and so the "real meaning" of literature in particular and art in general.[35] The novella recounts an attempt by two critics to figure out the true meaning of art after a contemporary novelist has informed them that they—and others like them—have missed his true intention:

> By my little point I mean—what shall I call it? The particular thing I've written my books most *for*. Isn't there for every writer a particular thing of

> that sort, the thing that most makes him apply himself, the thing without the effort to achieve which he wouldn't write at all, the very passion of his passion, the part of the business in which, for him, the flame of art burns most intensely? Well, it's *that*! (italics James), pp. 141–2

Contained here are but a few of the many figures of speech that the novelist and the other characters use to describe "it," the meaning that Hugh Vereker, the novelist in question, insists is missing from their and other critics' otherwise "clever" interpretations. Like the titular "figure in the carpet," many of these figures of speech involve a curious doubling: the "passion of one's passion," "the part of art where the flame burns most intensely," a "bird in a cage," "bait on a hook," the "string on which my pearls are strung," etc. In light of all these doublings, Vereker insists that the "figure in the carpet" is neither one nor the other but both; for example, it is neither content nor style but both—the most formal aspects of the work in question—including punctuation—as well as the most contentual. But why, when there are so many other figures to choose from, does James single out that of the "figure in the carpet"?

This figure must, in some way, hold the key to all the others. While I would agree with those who see in this important figure a reference to the figurative wovenness of "textuality" in general (the "carpet" as text, the text as carpet), or figuration in general (the "figure"), I think the answer is more concrete than that. With his choice of this particular figure for the truth of art, James/Vereker is saying that the "meaning" of art is always embedded in its concrete, material substance. However, this is not merely another materialist view of art, for the meaning of art is not this material substance, it is embedded "Deep Down" (the title of one of the novels mentioned in the story) in the "stuff" of art, be it "painting," or "film," or literature. As Heidegger noted in the Origin of Art essay (discussed later in this work), the peculiar fact that many forms of art refer to their material substance, rather than to any abstract idea, is indicative of this.[36] With this caveat, the so-called "meaning" of the work of art, or art in general, is synaesthetic in always bringing together word and image, or word and thing, "at the origin of both."[37] This is also what Heidegger means by arguing for art as returning us to the "thingness of the thing," not merely to the idea (word) or the thing, but to the origin (*Ursprung*) in which both are present together. The "figure in the carpet" is James' titular figure because it best reveals this synaesthetic meaning of all art.

But the other figures in James' novella—including the "figures" of the characters themselves, as well as the plot in which they are implicated—must also demonstrate this synaesthetic essence since, as the title suggests, the entire story of "the figure in the carpet" is "The Figure in the Carpet." When James doubles up figures like "the passion of my passion," the "part where the flame of art burns most intensely," etc., he is, in all these cases, asserting and denying at the same time the thing he is describing, because the material "thing" is always different from its idea; for example, the true passion of art is not passion as such but something that is and is not passion—it is passion going beyond itself as itself. In order to understand these figures less abstractly, it is important to acknowledge the synaesthetic essence of art as always exceeding itself as itself, the way a real synaesthete hears a color that is neither sound nor sight, but both simultaneously. In this regard it is important to note again that synaesthesia is not limited to any particular coupling, say, of hearing color or seeing sound, but can involve any number of different combinations whose common denominator is "crossing over" the usual separation between things.[38] To perform this operation successfully, and not merely to repeat the separation in crossing over, it is necessary to combine synaesthetically the "different" senses or, in the case of James' figure, the different senses of the word "passion."

In addition to the main plot of plumbing the depths of art there is another drama unfolding in James' novella involving the figures—or characters—in the story. The four principal characters, the two critics (George Corvick and the nameless narrator), Covick's fiancée Gwendolym Erme, and the famous artist in question, Hugh Vereker, constitute the four corners (*vier Ecken*?) of the story's "carpet," thus:

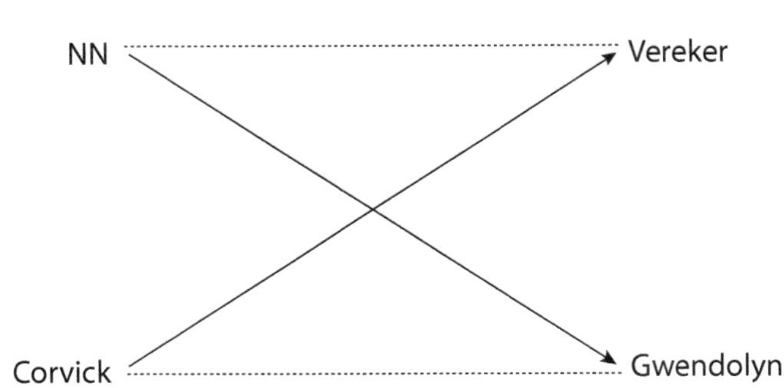

Figure 1.1 Miro, The Red Sun, 1948.

Why does Corvick succeed, and the nameless narrator fail? Corvick succeeds because he pursues the truth indirectly through something that is not what he is actually pursuing. This essential "disconnected connectedness" (what Fichte refers to as the necessary *hiatus irrationalis*—"irrational gap"—of the aesthetic absolute[39]) is made evident in a number of ways. First, there is the essential separation *and* connection between Corvick's simultaneous pursuit of Vereker and his pursuit of Gwendolyn. Second, we are told that he only discovers the answer to Vereker's secret when he leaves everything—Gwendolyn and Vereker's novels, and travels alone to India when, suddenly, the truth came out. Third, and perhaps most significantly, NN expresses his confusion—and ours—that whereas Gwendolyn informed him, after Corvick left for India, that they were definitely engaged to be married if and when Corvick figured out the secret, Corvick had expressly told him before leaving that they "were not a bit engaged." A "little point," as Vereker described his secret meaning, but also a very big one. What all these "disconnected connections" mean is not just that meaning is found where it is not, but that the truth of essential matters like the meaning of art and the meaning of true love (there is no question that Gwendolyn and George are an example of that) comes out in another form that is the same as, and different from, itself—the very definition of metaphor and of synaesthesia.

The nameless narrator fails at both these pursuits because of his extreme literal-mindedness. Throughout the novella he evinces his positivistic approach to things by insisting that Vereker stop using metaphors and state clearly what he means without ever stopping to consider what these metaphors might mean, including the ones we just discussed that occurred in the pivotal conversation between him and Vereker. Similarly, NN's attempt to win Gwendolyn in order to learn Vereker's secret is a crass attempt to "buy" the secret rather than understanding it as a synaesthetic "disconnected connection"—such prostitution is the epitome of what James typically decries as "vulgar." The final declaration of the novella, in which NN claims victory by discovering someone—Gwendolyn's second husband—who is even more benighted than he (who not only does not know the secret but also knows that he does not know it) is James' masterful way of saying that those who have lost their connection to the hidden, "disconnected connections" in life—disconnected connections that I am here labeling forms of synaesthesia—will never succeed in understanding art or, for that matter, love. In this respect, the positivistic NN (a recurrent "character type" in James' oeuvre[40]), is a version of ourselves—the literal, non-aesthetic, nonsynaesthetic part of all of us, more or less.

Synaesthesia, it will be argued here, is the key to understanding the "figure in the carpet." Even Hegel's famous notion of art as the "sensible appearance of the Idea" (*die sinnliche Erscheinung der Idee*) must be understood as referencing the synaesthetic embedding of an "idea" in a concrete thing and vice versa. Although this work will examine a number of modern artists who sometimes spoke explicitly about art's synaesthetic qualities, all "fine art" speaks a language that is not our ordinary language but, as Aristotle argued in the West's first work of literary theory, a language where the "greatest thing" (*to megiston*) is the metaphoric "crossing over" (*meta-pherein*) of something with what it is not.

Although Aristotle went on to define this process as the rational, ana-*logical* unity between two things, many later writers on the subject have insisted that in a genuine, poetic metaphor it is less the logical or analogical meaning that causes the poetic metaphor to work than the difference—Derrida's *différance*—between the two elements in question.[41] However, Derrida's (and others') notion of a difference that is always already different from itself in deferring its meaning outside of itself is still less logical than even this. For, in arguing that the "meaning" of art lies in its synaesthetic properties I hope to concretize this abstract formula of a "difference which is different from itself" as the sensory—rather than the merely (il)logical—unity between things.

Miró's Figure in the Carpet

Figure 1.2

If Henry James, in the story just discussed, was trying to get his audience to appreciate the figure in the carpet rather than the figure outside the carpet—that is to say, the figure as embedded, inseparably, within its concrete thing rather than outside it—then this representative painting of Miró's is precisely that. Here we see the other, non-reductive side of metaphor just mentioned, although, if I am right in identifying all art as metaphoric, it is also the other side of every genuine, poetic metaphor. When we use the term "surreal" to describe Miró's paintings we are merely using the language of this world to describe something other than this known world. But if we attempt to describe Miró's world in its own terms, this can only be done if we describe the work synaesthetically. But how does synaesthesia help us to talk about this painting? Or, more precisely, how is this painting already synaesthetic in ways that will help us to talk about it more concretely?

In a recent essay "On colored-hearing synaesthesia," Lawrence Marks proposes a new "connotative" theory of the experience in which "Synaesthesia is related to connotative meaning in general . . . certain synaesthetic relations (like pitch-brightness) are universal and *colors act as symbols*. The dimensions that underlie synaesthesia are the same as those that appear to underlie connotative meaning in general."[42] Pursuing such synaesthetic connotations we can start with the "conversation" that is taking place between the two-legged, officious figure standing in the lower-right portion of the painting with the otherwise still dominant figure in the field, the two-eyed, imbecilically smiling red figure who is listening to this more grounded fellow on the lower-right (he is the only one occupying a grounded, horizontal position), who is droning on in the official language of that figure, appropriately dressed in his more formal, black attire—more formal, that is, than the unleashed red circle that is directly to the left of the imbecilic figure who is responding to the officious one.

The officious figure might certainly be likened to Franco, particularly when one considers Picasso's well-known—and most certainly well-known to Miró—caricatures of Franco that resemble this figure.[43] Indeed, most discussions of Miró, here and, particularly, in Spain where the presence of Franco is still ubiquitous, note how the Spanish dictator's presence is also ubiquitous in the Catalan painter's work. But, now that the two principal players of Miró's drama have been identified, let us see what the other figures in the carpet have to say. (As one might expect, many of Miró's paintings were made into tapestries, but the fact that they are already tapestries might be why such works—as opposed to Miró's sculptures--seem redundant.)

To the right of "Franco" is a very small figure that is analogous to the blackened "imbecilic" red figure and its freer counterpart, the unbounded red figure to its left, even to the point of also being enclosed within an azure opening that we have yet to address. The final, fourth iteration of these red/black figures is in the olive-green "leaf" at the bottom of the azure opening, a figure that, with the single line that curves around it (the only such line in the painting, if one excludes those forming the "mustache" of our imbecile), resembles a sort of pet lying at the feet of its "master," although it might also be accompanying "Franco." Either way, the microcosmic version of the figure to Franco's right is a warning to the larger figure of what will happen to it if the dictator has his way.

Finally, excluded from this "human" drama are the large azure opening itself and the many blotches of color (more green, yellow, orange, a deeper blue, white, etc.) that intermingle with black in the form of loose, incomplete borders (most notable around the large darker blue blotch) and rather amorphous ink "drips." These black "drips," in being consistently unlike the other, more complete black figures discussed—most notably, the dictator, but also surrounding the fool—and being consistently placed within the azure window, represent the opening to freedom itself, the sky, the sea, whatever is as of yet unbounded by the law (which is always "black and white," never in color), just as the large unbounded red orb—half in, half out of the picture—seems destined to be surrounded by the law once it has made its way into the opening to freedom.

Before one dismisses this reading as itself an "imbecilic" regression to a greatly outdated personification of nonhuman forms, let me say that I agree that what has been said thus far is *not* what this great painting is about. It is ultimately free from this just as the painting itself is free from dictatorial behests of the "law" that I see represented in the painting—the painting, in other words, is ultimately free from the law it portrays just as the figures are free from "Franco." The point of my *reading* is that the painting synaesthetically *speaks* to us, not in any literal, definitive way, but as a catachresis that gives us a different sense—in both senses of the word—than just sight or sound, image or word, by itself. Catachresis, one will recall, is a "true falsity" because it gives us a figure from another sense for something that does not have its own name or meaning. The importance of synaesthesia in grounding this abstract notion is that it explains why the meaning of art is always catachrestic and always allegorical (*allos agoreuein*—speaking otherwise—for example, "in tongues"): before meaning has become objective and literal, it has always already crossed over into another sense or meaning that is more original than the "original," literal meaning.[44]

Paintings speak, and we shall attempt, throughout this volume, to hear what other painters—such as Klee, Picasso, O'Keeffe, Mitchell, and Rouault—as well as various artworks, artists, and philosophers are saying. This does not mean that we will engage in trite, allegorical interpretations of what the painting, or musical work, or poem means. For this synaesthetic version of "word and image studies"—which is more properly defined as word *as* image studies—is based on the premise that the "origin of the work of art," that which makes it original, lies in a synaesthetic unity that proceeds the identification of the work with something more literal or objectively real. For this reason, the synaesthetic "crossings" can take many different forms, such as in the music of certain paintings by O'Keeffe (the "music of flowers"), the "story" one can read by following the "narrative" of Picasso's Vollard Suite, the "smell" of Francis Bacon,[45] the musical meaning of "nonsensical" pop lyrics, the modern "gospel" of overtly religious works such as those of Rouault, the tactile truth of cubism, movie/music, etc.

What all these studies have in common, and what they have in common with James' and Miró's figures "in the carpet," is that they all demonstrate the thesis that art is originally synaesthetic. This is the secret meaning of art that, according to James, has been largely overlooked in our all-too-human understanding of art in nonsynaesthetic terms.

2

"Deep Down": Metaphor as Synaesthetic[1]

To argue that metaphor is synaesthetic in always "crossing over" (the literal definition of metaphor) from one thing to another, or from one sense to another, would probably not encounter much resistance. Similarly, to say that all art is metaphorical would not be difficult to prove, however much the more literal-minded thinker might insist upon the realism or objective truth of art. But to say that all art is essentially synaesthetic because all metaphor is synaesthetic and all art is metaphoric, however logically necessary that conclusion might be, is a more difficult argument to make. Our focus here will be on demonstrating, first, the synaesthetic nature of metaphor, and then that this synaesthetic basis of metaphor leads to the synaesthetic nature of all art. This beginning chapter will thus also serve to clarify an essential question forever lurking in the background of this project and to which we will have numerous occasions to return, namely, that of the relationship between artistic synaesthesia and real, "neurological" synaesthesia.

Metaphor as Synaesthetic

Although there have been repeated attempts to understand metaphor ever since Aristotle first defined it as the illicit "reference to something using a word that belongs to something else" (*epiphora onomatos allotriou*), the general consensus now, at least among many literary theorists and philosophers, is that a particular metaphor, or metaphor in general, cannot be defined since, in "crossing over" from one thing to another, any definition that stops this motion must inevitably fail to describe it: "The metaphorization of metaphor, it's bottomless overdeterminability, seems to be written into the structure of metaphor, though as its negative side."[2] Needless to say, and as the quote from Paul de Man above succinctly states, there is a great deal at stake in this controversy, for the movement of metaphor, which is also necessarily a metaphor of movement, is extremely vexing to those who insist on proper definitions for things even when the very notion of "propriety," another term for the literal, is explicitly excluded from the very thing one seeks to define.

Among those willing to accept the problematical—or, in the words of Cleanth Brooks, *paradoxical*[3]—nature of metaphor, there is agreement that every attempted definition of metaphor is also a metaphor of a definition and, furthermore, that every particular poetic metaphor is also a metaphor of itself—a double "metaphor of metaphor," if you will.[4] All "living," poetic metaphors, for which Paul Ricoeur coined the term "*métaphores vives*"[5] can only be defined or known in terms that are belied by the metaphor itself, and are therefore metaphors of the original metaphor, however apt that explanatory metaphor might be. And this applies also to the terms used to describe or explain metaphor in general, which are also inevitably metaphoric. For example, in the aforementioned definition Aristotle refers to a "carrying" or "borrowing" from one word to another that does not, of course, literally occur. And this infestation of metaphors by other metaphors also applies to those metaphors that have ceased to be "living" and have become examples of the countless unpoetical metaphors that make up much of our daily speech—"I see what you mean," "That is crazy," "Far out," "Cold-blooded," "Hot topic," etc. We call such terms whose metaphoricity has been forgotten "dead metaphors," a reminder that even references to metaphors that are no longer metaphors are now, metaphorically, "deceased."

Considerable, if metaphorical, light may be shone on particular metaphors as well as on the various theories of metaphor by approaching this convoluted matter in terms of synaesthesia. While there are few references to synaesthesia among writers on metaphor, there are numerous references to metaphor among those writing on the subject of synaesthesia. V. S. Ramachandran "finds in the artist-synesthete an unusual ability to blend realities, employ the power of metaphor," while the painter Franz Kupka, like other members of the Orphic circle, wavered between a distrust of literal, "organic" synaesthesia ("The eye has no sense of harmony in the same meaning as the ear. There is no music to the eye") and a passionate embrace of its metaphorical counterpart: "Kupka . . . continued to value the abiding power of musical metaphors. He transformed the specifically musical analogy of pure painting into a vitalist theory of natural vibration."[6] However, other than noting the obvious general connection between metaphorical "cross overs" and synaesthesia, neither those dealing with synaesthesia "proper" nor those writing on metaphor have taken this accepted but unexplored connection as seriously as the psychologist Lawrence Marks, who "has argued that the two [metaphor and synaesthesia] have a common basis in the brain."[7] "Real synaesthetes" reject the connection to metaphor because, for them, the connections are literal—a color *does* have a sound, or an odor, etc., while the many theorists of metaphor are content to relegate metaphor to the paradigmatic realm of related ideas (or "pseudo-ideas") that have no relation to the concrete, sensible realities that compose *la métaphore vive*, the "living metaphor." Even the latter defenders of the "metaphorization of metaphor" are in reality detractors of metaphor if they fail to acknowledge the concrete synaesthetic reality that is the very raison d'etre of metaphor. We shall first revisit, then, Nietzsche's famous description of the process whereby "original metaphors" are poetically weakened as they devolve over time into "dead metaphors" as an example of one of these important modern and/or postmodern theories that nonetheless fails to refer metaphor back to its original, synaesthetic "essence."

Nietzsche and Metaphor

Nietzsche's most extensive, and most important discussion of metaphor occurs in his famous unpublished early essay of 1872, "On Truth and Lies in an Extra-moral Sense," the text to which Sara Kofman devotes almost the entirety of her book *Nietzsche and Metaphor*.[8] The importance of this essay in foreshadowing many of Nietzsche's major ideas cannot be overstated, but we will focus here on those parts of this essay related directly, or indirectly, to his statements regarding metaphor.

"Only by means of forgetfulness can man ever arrive at imagining that he possesses 'truth.'"[9] Nietzsche's striking notion of a "forgetfulness"

(*Vergessenheit*) that constitutes the remembering of consciousness—a reversal that will also find its way into the very essence of psychoanalysis—is one of the major themes of this essay, and although it might not appear at first to be related to metaphoricity, Nietzsche will makes this connection explicit later in the essay when he states:

> What therefore is truth? A mobile army of metaphors, metonymies, anthropomorphisms: in short a sum of human relations which became poetically and rhetorically intensified, metamorphosed, adorned, and after long usage seem to a nation fixed, canonic and binding; *truths are illusions of which one has forgotten that they are illusions*; worn-out metaphors which have become powerless to affect the senses; coins with their images effaced and now no longer of account as coins but merely as metal. (italics mine)

If one follows Nietzsche's logic carefully one realizes that there are, in fact, two different "truths" referred to here and throughout the essay. The first, or the second chronologically speaking, is the illusion of knowing something to be true. From the beginning of his essay Nietzsche has made it clear that "possession" of this truth is in fact "arrogance" (*Hochmuth*) and "ignorance" (*Nichtwissen*) in its defensive insistence upon a certainty that is based on an insecure uncertainty. One cannot help but compare this to Descartes' desperate attempts to reverse the Copernican revolution by establishing a new center, a self-proclaimed "Archimedean point" of truth in, of all things, reason itself. (Nietzsche's version of this can be found in the opening paragraph, where he derides our supposed cosmological centering as comparable to the gnat which "feels within itself the flying center of the world.") If, as Nietzsche proclaims, this "truth" is anything but true, there is yet another "Truth" that can be discerned here, although, for reasons that are quite logically consistent, that Truth is perhaps not really truth in the other sense at all. In the passage just quoted the term "Wahrheit" can also refer to the metaphoric "illusion that one has NOT forgotten is an illusion" and so is, like the metaphor of "taste" in art, a catachrestic "true illusion." This is, to be sure, a very different kind of truth.

Nietzsche does not say "What then is truth? Metaphors, metonymies, etc." but, rather, "What then is truth? A *moving army* (*bewegliches Heer*) of metaphors, metonymies, etc." Notwithstanding Nietzsche's oft-times bellicose nature, the reference to a "moving army" is clearly false or, better, illusory. Indeed, not only is the reference to an army metaphorical, but even the reference to motion—and time—is illusory insofar as one cannot really know anything about time and motion without turning them into something they are not. In any case, in using an illusory metaphor to "define" the metaphorical process of Truth—the other kind of truth—Nietzsche has offered as an alternative to logical truth (A = A) something that is true because it is not true. *Thus the catachrestic "moving army" is synaesthetic in not being an idea as such but, rather, a sensuous, synaesthetic Truth that lies at the basis of art as a truth that is no more.*

Although it is often assumed that Nietzsche is opposing an original "poetic" vision of things to a more pedestrian, logical knowledge of the same, that is not quite true in that the process of "poetic and rhetorical intensification" occurs later, as a "translation" of the original Truth, thus already beginning the metaphorical process whereby the Truth has lost its original currency. The original original "Truth," as it were, occurs before there is any metaphor per se. It is, to be as precise as possible, always already forgotten. But it is not nothing, for to say that would be to remember—and forget—it in perhaps the most logical, contradictory terms of all. It is our humanity ("a sum of human relations") that speaks through the poetic metaphors which, while not the truth, represent the synaesthetic truth that we are (not).

Nietzsche himself provides one such metaphor of our deeper, synaesthetic essence earlier in the essay when he tells us what he believes humanity truly is. The description may surprise you:

> What indeed does man know about himself! Is he able even once to see himself complete, placed as it were in an illuminated glass case? Does not nature keep secret from him most things, even about his body . . . so as to banish and lock him up in proud, fraudulent knowledge? Nature threw away the key; and woe to the fateful curiosity (*wehe der verhängnissvollen Neubegier*) which might be able for a moment to look out and down through a crevice in the chamber of consciousness, and discover that man, in the careless indifference of his ignorance, is resting on what is ruthless, voracious, insatiable, and murderous, and, as it were, hanging in dreams on the back of a tiger. (89)

It is not that "we are the glass men," itself a powerful metaphor for our world of sterile, fraudulent knowledge, but, rather, that the glass case of knowledge is exactly that, a case containing an unknown, living, breathing being—unknown because, in our so-called knowledge of our own existential reality, we efface that very reality. That reality is something very different, but, again, before we are too quick to respond with Nietzsche's metaphor of the tiger, we note that it is not the tiger to which humanity itself is being compared but, rather, a fractured "moment" (*einmal*) in which we merely "suspect" (*ahnen*) that humanity (*der Mensch*) is resting (*ruhen*) on an animalistic ruthlessness (*dem Unersättlichsten, dem Mörderischen*, etc.) that is unconscious and (so) indifferent (*in der Gleichgültigkeit seines Nichtwissens*), "*like hanging on the back of a tiger in our dreams*" (*gleichsam auf dem Rücken eines Tigers in Träumen hängend*). The metaphorical (*gleichsam*) tiger reference is clearly parallel to the earlier reference to an indifferent ruthless, murderous voracity that humanity "rests upon" (*ruhe auf*), just as, here, it "hangs from the back" of a tiger—the parallel is even clearer in German given the similar sounding terms *ruhen* and *Rücken*. The higher truth of who we really are, then, is not the rather banal comparison to the "beast within" but, rather, to a dreamlike movement of moments from which mankind is always, temporally speaking, "lagging" or, spatially speaking, "lacking" or, to combine both, "hanging back." The murderousness is not, then, really murderousness per se or, again, the cliché of bestial violence but, more subtly, a synaesthetic mind/body, human/animal synthesis that maintains a separation between the two at the very moment that the two are conjoined. In other words: "the animal that therefore I am" (Derrida) is also "the animal that therefore I am not," just as the synaesthetic metaphorical reality of who we are—which is exactly what Nietzsche is describing here—is also not the reality of who we therefore are.

We are also perhaps too quick in rushing past the beginning of this description of our synaesthetic, metaphorical being if we ignore the contempt with which Nietzsche describes this "discovery," for "fateful curiosity" (*verhängnissvollen Neubegier*) is not a phrase that suggests approval on Nietzsche's part. Indeed, one might compare this description to Nietzsche's contemptuous dismissal of Schiller's famous "Veil of Isis" poem,[10] which ends with a similar "Woe to he who . . . " warning. In Nietzsche's discussion of that poem that appears at the end of the second Preface of 1886 to the *Fröhliche Wissenschaft* ("Joyful Science"), Nietzsche derides, as Schiller himself does but for very different reasons, the young man whose own "fateful curiosity" led him to lift the Veil of Isis to see the Absolute or "All." While Schiller condemns the young man's efforts on moral grounds, Nietzsche warns against such peering into the ultimate truth of things because he everywhere rejects the romantic, Faustian striving for the absolute on the grounds of its necessary contradiction—humans simply can't "know" or "see" (both Nietzsche and Schiller use *sehen*) an absolute that exceeds, by definition, the very thing-in-itself that is being posited. But does this make of Nietzsche, then, a "positivist," or "empiricist" who rejects metaphysics altogether? And who rejects the synaesthetic, versus aesthetic, oneness that underlies the veil of Isis?

Hardly. When Nietzsche warns against the "potentially disastrous curiosity" that would lead one to see the way things really are, it is because the way things really are is not really anything at all. That is to say, the absolute cannot maintain the separation between things or the senses, which is a function of the logical filtering of consciousness; as Nietzsche says of the "pure Dionysian," it cannot exist because it cannot exist as such. But the obvious connection between the synaesthetic absolute and the Dionysian warns us against turning Nietzsche into any kind of positivistic anti-Dionysian. What Nietzsche is really rejecting is not the Dionysian "All" but, rather, the way one goes about pursuing it. One recalls, as an example of this, Nietzsche's distinction, in *The Birth of Tragedy*, between an "Aryan" challenge to the separation between God and man represented by Prometheus and a "Semitic" version of this same challenge that takes the form of mere "curiosity" as described in Eve's temptation to becoming a god herself. It is not the synaesthetic absolute that Nietzsche rejects but the metaphysical positing of it as such that, in talking about art, in talking about metaphorical synaesthesia, in talking about the absolute, unavoidably turns art into "aesthetics," metaphor into an Aristotelian analogy, and synaesthesia into mere "intra-sensory associations."

Nietzsche is not rejecting the metaphorical, synaesthetic absolute but redefining it in post-romantic terms as what it truly is (not). Adherence to the Dionysian, synaesthetic absolute is, indeed, what Nietzsche means by adherence to the earth as our constant reminder of a separation between words, and between the senses, whose falsity is the very definition of a truth that is not "beyond truth and lies."

Heidegger: Synaesthesia as the Metaphorical Ground of Being

"Ground," in Heidegger's magisterial treatise *Der Satz vom Grund*, "The Principle of Reason," refers to the essential principle of the modern, post-Copernican world, the rational principal enunciated by Leibniz that "Everything has a reason," or "Nihil est sine ratione" ("Nothing is without reason"). For something, anything, to be, it must be something that can be understood as having a reason, whether that reason be a "cause" outside itself or, more generally speaking, an adequate logical explanation (*ratio sufficiens.*) However, this "principle of reason" that mandates that there be an adequate explanation for everything has, itself, no rational, or even adequate, explanation; thus, the explanatory power of this principle—and it is, to be sure, enormously powerful—is powerless to explain the basis of its own power. "Nothing is without a reason" except, it seems, this very principle, for the "cause of the cause," as it were, the basis for the basis of everything does not itself have any logical explanation. I can explain everything but that I can explain everything, just as I cannot explain why there is anything, including the explaining self, rather than nothing. It is telling that the "mere metaphor" of the "ground" points to the very nonexistence—nothing—of the "ground" itself.

Why, and how, should one concern oneself with this underlying "ungrounded ground" of things, given its own inaccessibility to the very "law of the ground" that it establishes "for us" but which is, itself, separate "from us" in being "in itself"? With regards to the "why," which is the easier question to answer, the Being (*Sein*) that underlies particular beings (*Seienden*) is important for the same reason that it is unimportant; that is, as that which ultimately or originally causes the very existence of causes it remains critically important because, not despite, of the fact that it is itself outside the very principle it creates. That principle, the Leibnizian notion of a rational "accounting" that must be rendered by every being (as Heidegger reminds us, "account in Latin is called *ratio*" 119), is no more complete than the various "accounts" one is expected to render in so many different aspects of our lives, all of them rational (e.g., "How many books do you own?" as opposed to "How many books do you understand?" or "How many books have you written?" as opposed to "What is their importance, if any?"). So much for the "why" we are inevitably if reluctantly drawn to the Being of beings; "how" to access this originary truth, and what this has to do with *metaphor* (which Heidegger explicitly discusses in this book) and *synaesthesia* (which he does not) remains to be seen.

"Tone," or "Intonation" is frequently invoked in Lecture VI of *The Principle of Being*, the lecture (there are thirteen in all, as well as a summary address (*Vortrag*) that Heidegger gave during the same term in 1956) that contains the explicit discussion of metaphor. The double "principle of the principle of reason," the truth about the principle of reason, is not understandable in terms of itself, for then it would be a mere principle of reason rather than the principle of the principle of reason, which must be different. Rather, Heidegger insists, it can only be "understood" if one hears it with the proper intonation, for "thinking should bring into view something one has already heard *in the intonation*. . . . In so doing it brings into view what was un-heard of . . . therefore, in thinking both ordinary hearing and seeing pass away for us" (46-7). A curious, almost chemical reaction occurs when one doubles certain words such as, here, the "principle of principle(s)," for that results in something that both is and is not itself—for example, here, the "principle of principle" is a principle but it is also something else, something that is therefore both inside and outside itself at the same time. As anomalous as such a pattern might seem, it is the very model of "aesthetic figuration" as it consistently presents itself outside itself; as opposed to Plato's "itself according to itself," it is that which "denies itself as such."[11]

If Heidegger chooses to emphasize the sound, or intonation, of this double "principle of principle" rather than its necessarily ambiguous, aporistic meaning, he is not referring to the sound of "principle" but to its intonation, which is, as he insists, tonally and totally different. Heidegger is not referring to the importance of hearing as pure sound any more than he is referring to an "ordinary hearing," which merely assumes an unproblematic relationship between the two, between pure sound that we supposedly hear and the pure meaning that we supposedly don't. Proper hearing, or as Jean-Luc Nancy defines it, listening,[12] is neither sound nor meaning but both. It is, with regard to its relation to the curious pattern of doubling we just described, outside itself in being and not being what it is. It is also, in Heidegger's words, a seeing and a thinking ("Thinking should bring into view something one has already heard in the intonation") or, in other words, synaesthesia.

But if Heidegger identifies the real "principle of reason," the "principle of principle(s)," with its sound and even its sight, why, then, does he seemingly reject the metaphoricity of this same experience when metaphor seemingly provides the synaesthetic unity of sight/sound and thinking he identifies with true Being? For it is the case that Heidegger, who is certainly not someone who has a "deaf hear" when it comes to poetry, nonetheless seems to reject metaphoricity when he writes:

> Because our hearing and seeing is never a mere sensible registering, it is therefore also off the mark to insist that thinking as listening and bringing-into-view are only meant as . . . transposing the supposedly sensible into the nonsensible. The idea of "transposing" and of metaphor is based upon the distinguishing, if not complete separation, of the sensible and the nonsensible as two realms that subsist on their own. . . . When one gains the insight into the limitations of metaphysics, "metaphor" as a normative conception also becomes untenable—that is to say that metaphor is the norm for our conception of the essence of language. Thus metaphor serves as a handy crutch in the interpretation of works of poetry and of artistic production in general. The metaphorical exists only within metaphysics. (48)

I would argue that it is precisely because metaphor *is* the synaesthetic unity between thought, sound, and sight that Heidegger rejects *metaphoricity*, *not* metaphor, as a "normative conception" of metaphor. For metaphoricity is not real poetic metaphor but, rather, the idea of a poetics (more precisely, Aristotle's *Poetics*—the first and still foremost argument for the importance of metaphoricity) in which what is concealed in a poetic metaphor is itself concealed by a definition that would define a particular metaphor or metaphor in general as the translation or "transposing" from the sensible into thought (e.g., "my love is like a red, red rose") rather than as the unity between the sensible and thought that remains hidden from view because it is both seen and heard and thought. This is why, I would argue, the Scottish poet says "red" twice, for the intonation denies the simple elevation from the sensible to the ideal. This reduction of metaphor to its logical truth that began with

Aristotle ignores the metaphoricity of its own definition and emphasizes, instead, the literalness of metaphor, the very thing that denies the literal. It is this Aristotelian defacement of metaphor in the name of metaphoricity that Heidegger condemns, not the illogical synaesthetic unity of metaphor that remains concealed in every genuine poetic metaphor, something that Aristotle tries to avoid by using mostly "dead metaphors" (sc. logical metaphors) in the *Poetics* but which nonetheless resurfaces in his own "metaphors of metaphor" and in his reluctant inclusion of catachrestic metaphors that seemingly deny, or attenuate, metaphor's nonsynaesthetic logic.

Although Heidegger insists that the concept of metaphor—"metaphoricity"—is inherently metaphysical in returning meaning to itself via its transferences from the sensible to sense, he was not thereby rejecting metaphor in its own metaphoricity—the "metaphor of metaphor"—but, rather, he was rejecting the subsumption (Derrida refers this to the Hegelian notion of "sublation") of the *sensible* as such to *sense* as such. That is to say, "metaphoricity" is actually a denial of metaphor if one defines metaphor in general or a particular metaphor as meaning, in particular if one denies the very separation from meaning that is the very essence of metaphor and the sensible, as opposed to metaphor "as such" or the sensible "as such." When one hears, according to Heidegger, one does not hear hearing, which is all one hears if one assumes the "metaphysical" position of the reduction of the sensible to its sense. Thus, Heidegger's criticism of metaphoricity as metaphysical ("The metaphorical exists only within metaphysics," 48) applies only to the general notion, or sense, of metaphor rather than to the non-sensical, non-grounded denial of meaning as such in every "living" metaphor, just as Heidegger's negative view of the "metaphysical" tradition is in no way a rejection of Being (*Sein*), which Heidegger, especially in his later works, identifies with artistic truth—that is, with living, poetic metaphors. And so, just as Heidegger's notion of this artistic, non-"metaphysical" revelation of Being is inherently syn-aesthetic (as opposed to "aesthetic") in its denial of any being as such, metaphor (vs. metaphoricity) is inherently synaesthetic in crossing over from the sensible to sense without returning meaning to itself. In other words, **the metaphysical metaphorics of aesthetics need be replaced by the absolute metaphor of syn-aesthetics**.

Derrida: "White Mythology"

Although Derrida does not refer to synaesthesia in either of his two essays on metaphor (nor, I believe, anywhere in his prolific writings), I would like to show that what he is describing as the "deconstruction" of metaphor is synaesthetic in its very essence—understanding that what is essential is not the same as what is meaningful. One can argue, as Derrida does, that metaphor is essentially "double" in denying its own meaning, or in doubling the "sense" of meaning with the "sense" of the sensory that, curiously, gives meaning its meaning ("this divergence between sense (signified) and the senses (sensible signifier) is declared through the same root (*sensus, Sinn*)"[13]), but one can also go deeper than this abstract formulation by reversing the usual hierarchy of sense over the senses with the synaesthetic hierarchy of the senses over sense. For example, in a true poetic metaphor like Homer's reference to Apollo as descending upon the Greeks at Troy "*hos nukti*," "like the night," (*Iliad*, Bk. I) it is not Apollo or night per se that is at work here but, rather, the absolute, synaesthetic unity of both.

This deeper, synaesthetic experience of metaphor is not, however, altogether absent in Derrida's treatment of metaphor in the first of his two essays on the subject, *White Mythology (Mythologie blanche)*. In the final pages of his essay he turns from the "philosophical form" of metaphor (what Heidegger had referred to as the implication of metaphoricity in its metaphysical "sense" or understanding) to a "second form of self-destruction of metaphor [that] is deceptively similar to the philosophical form":

> The second form of self-destruction of metaphor is deceptively similar to the philosophical form. It follows the first closely, but is there as an additional element of syntactic resistance, arising from everything (for example in modem linguistics) which thwarts the distinction between syntax and semantics, and above all the philosophical hierarchy in which syntax is subordinated to semantics. Self-destruction here still has the form of generalization, but in this case it is not a matter of extending and confirming a philosophical notion, but rather of deploying it in such a way, without limit, that the borders of what is proper for it are tom from it; consequently the reassuring dichotomy between the metaphorical and the proper is

> exploded, that dichotomy in which each member of the pair never did more than reflect the other and direct back its radiance. Metaphor, then, always has its own death within it. (pp. 73–4; underlining mine)

The "syntactical resistance" Derrida is referring to, "for example in modern linguistics," is the resistance—or, in the terms of the next essay to be discussed, the "retreat"—of metaphor to its semantic significance; that is, to the supposed separation by Jakobson and other modern, structural linguists of metaphor from metonymy, of the paradigmatic "axis of comparison" from the syntagmatic axis of spatiotemporal "contiguity." The problem with this structural "hierarchy" or separation is that the "other metaphor" deconstructs, or "self-destructs" this opposition by the denial of this meaning (the "death of metaphor") *and* the meaning of this denial. For example, in the Homeric metaphor or simile just mentioned (and what is a simile if not a reminder of this syntactical "différance?"), Apollo's baleful destruction of the Greeks is neither the night or not the night, it is a metaphor/metonymy in which the two are a true double, neither one nor two, but both. One is left, then, with a "radiance" or (in the words of the great comparatist René Wellek, "illumination") between two things that are syn-aesthetically, as opposed to just aesthetically, one. (One might also think of the "radiance" that Kafka's "man from the country" sees just before he is about to die and finally escape his "human condition" of being always "before the law.")

This second, "other metaphor," which one might also refer to as the "metaphor of the other" because of its inherent difference from itself, "carries its death within it" just as every living metaphor carries a "dead metaphor" within it. This second, "other metaphor" is, then, a flower, a "flower of rhetoric" in which what blooms is "without why," for it has no reason outside nor, for that matter, inside itself.

> Such a flower always bears within itself its own double, whether it be the seed or the type, the chance of its program or the necessity of its diagram. The heliotrope may always raise itself up. And it may always become a dried flower in a book. There is always, absent from any garden, a dried flower in a book ; and because of the repetition in which it is endlessly spoilt, no language can bring within its compass the structure of an anthology. Anthology is powerless before this supplemented code in

> which the field is crossed, the fences endlessly shifted, the line confused, the circle opened. (p. 74)

"Anthology," literally a "collection of flowers" (with emphasis on the "logic" of this) is "powerless" before the flower's living existence as such, a "living metaphor" in which what arises is "always already" grounded in its own groundlessness, its own "without why." And this tropological movement away from its own ground is what makes every metaphor a trope of itself, a "metaphor of metaphor" in which the senses inherently collide in a synaesthetic transference that carries its "anthological" meaning away from itself into itself, just as, for example, a flower becomes a painting, a lithograph, or even a stone:

> An anthology [is] also a lithography. Indeed, the heliotrope is a stone too: a precious stone, greenish and veined with red, a kind of Eastern jasper.

Derrida: "The Retreat of Metaphor"

Metaphor, like music, does not really exist. It is this nonexistent existence that results in the statement by Heidegger that seemed to turn against metaphor and reject it as merely a function of the false metaphysical separation of thinking from the senses, of intellectual reason from concrete, material existence. Just as music is lost the moment it is thought of as such or reasoned as such and such a thing, metaphor is lost just as soon as it is thought of as such or conceptualized. For metaphor, like music, always precedes the thought that would attempt to crystallize, dissect, or define it. For this reason one can say, as Heidegger does implicitly and Derrida explicitly, that all definitions of metaphor, whether of this or that metaphor specifically or metaphor in general (metaphoricity), are metaphors of definitions and thus false "catachreses" of a truth that cannot be otherwise defined. In examining Derrida's return to metaphor in this second essay we will attempt to relate his argument here, as we did with his earlier argument in "White Mythology," to a deeper level of synaesthetic experience that underlies both Heidegger's and Derrida's writings on metaphor.

Although, as just mentioned, Derrida is more "forgiving" of metaphor than Heidegger in carefully delimiting what we have referred to as "metaphoricity" from the metaphor as such, with the former being part of our metaphysical tradition in defining metaphor as a "sensible idea," Heidegger's awareness of the distinction between "living," poetic metaphors, and any theoretical understanding of such is clearly evident in this passage, in which Derrida quotes Heidegger quoting Hölderlin:

> "Wir blieben in der Metaphysik hängen, wollten wir dieses nennen Hölderlins in der Wendung 'Worte wie Blumen' für eine Metapher halten."
>
> ("We remain stuck in metaphysics if we take Hölderlin's 'turn of phrase' (nennen in der Wendung) 'words like flowers' for a metaphor.")[14]

Here Heidegger is distinguishing between what is clearly a metaphor from taking this very thing as a metaphor—between, if you will, the first "as" ("wie") from the second "as" in which we double the "words like flowers" with the second "like words like flowers" in which, as a necessary consequence of this debilitating redundancy, we identify or name ("nennen") as metaphor the simple "trope" ("Wendung") that Hölderlin used for "words as flowers." This difference is at once insignificant and profound. On the one hand, identifying Hölderlin's trope as a metaphor, which it clearly is, is merely to restate the obvious. On the other hand, by retreating from the original trope and identifying it *as* a metaphor the trope withdraws from an identification that is not a metaphor as such but, in this case, the synaesthetic reality of words (as) flowers. And, we might add, since we don't really know what language is by virtue of being locked up within language (one can't define what is already part of the defining rather than just the definition), Holderlin's original, tropic, poetic understanding of language as flowers is closer to the truth of language despite, or rather by virtue of, being a metaphor.

It is not, as we have stated before, that Heidegger rejects metaphor but, rather, that metaphor rejects us; that is, metaphor retreats—withdraws—whenever we try to grasp it as such. It is for this reason that Heidegger (as also Derrida) rejects metaphoricity but not metaphor. But to speak of the withdrawal of metaphor when this withdrawal itself withdraws from the truth of metaphor is, as the very term implies, an ab-straction from the concrete experience of the wholeness of metaphor, a concrete wholeness which we hope to describe more positively as syn-aesthesia, whether synaesthesia is taken literally or, as we have done throughout this treatise, figuratively as the figurative truth of art in general. If, as Derrida argues, metaphor necessarily withdraws in its concrete presence, then must it not also be the case that, since this withdrawal is a non-metaphor-metaphor in being the catachrestic truth of metaphor that is neither literal nor figurative ("the expression 'withdrawal of Being' is not *stricto sensu* metaphoric" (p. 67)), is it not also the case that metaphor exists in a synaesthetic reality that can never be known as such, but that can be experienced "aesthetically" as that which can never be known as such?

Derrida also discusses another metaphor that, like the "withdrawal" of metaphor, is not a metaphor "*in stricto sensu*," because it is a catachresis that, in describing something that can only be described metaphorically, is literal as well as metaphoric. Here I again quote Derrida quoting Heidegger, this time from his famous "Letter on Humanism":

> The talk about the house of Being (*Die Rede vom Haus des Seins*) is no transfer (*Übertragung*) of the image "house" to Being. But one day we will, by thinking the essence of Being, more readily be able to think what "house" and "to dwell" are. (p. 69)

Here it is very clear that Heidegger does not reject metaphor but metaphor "as such" if it is not essential, if it is merely a "transference" (*Übertragung*) from one term to the other. To speak of the "House of Being" *is* both metaphysical and metaphorical although it is neither metaphysical nor metaphorical as such. In other words, there is no "as such" when the thing one is describing (here, our relation to Being as opposed to beings) is essentially metaphorical. It is for this reason that Derrida notes that it is not so much a matter of merely thinking Being as a house as it is of also thinking the house as Being, for, that way, one avoids literalizing anything in this extraordinary statement. With this caveat in mind one realizes that Being is a "house" before there are any houses as such. Being is a house because it is both inside and outside us as our incessant search for a totality that both precedes and follows us wherever and whenever we are. It is necessarily metaphorical because the literal can only reside within it. It is necessarily synaesthetic because the "house of Being" is also not a house, it is something uncanny, "not of the house" (*un-heimliches*), that only finds itself where it is not, just as synaesthesia is always uncanny in reminding us of a preexistent unity that is the origin—the house—of whatever we know nonmetaphorically, "as such."

3

The Synaesthetic *Origin of the Work of Art*

Following our discussion of metaphor as synaesthesia, in which we used writings by Heidegger and Derrida to support our argument, we will now examine two different essays by these same philosophers that, like the preceding works, do not discuss synaesthesia per se but nonetheless demonstrate the importance of understanding art in general synaesthetically: Heidegger's essay on *The Origin of the Work of Art* and Jacques Derrida's essay on *Memories of the Blind.*[1] The first work is justly famous and needs no introduction; the second, more recent work deals with a selection of drawings from the Louvre that the philosopher uses to explain his remarkable thesis that painting is not really visual but, rather, made for and by the blind. Both works, coincidentally, are similar ventures into the realm of aesthetics by philosophers whose works are usually concerned with non-aesthetic matters, but for whom the aesthetic is qualitatively, if not quantitatively, of the highest importance in their respective *oeuvres*. Indeed, that the crossover between art and philosophy is, I would maintain, the highest form of art's synaesthetic ontology is demonstrated in the third, "epilogue" section of this chapter, which brings both philosophers together in an analysis of their writings on the synaesthetic nature of friendship.

The Origin of the Work of Art

The genius of Heidegger's writings is that they always take the form of a questioning that rigorously refuses to accept the commonly held answers and "truths," which blind us to the very truths they mean to explain. It is not surprising, then, that this hermeneutical, circular questioning that reveals less about what we know and more about what—positively—we don't know is readily apparent in Heidegger's most famous essay on art:

> Another way in which truth occurs is the act that founds a political state. Still another way in which truth comes to shine forth is the nearness of that which is not simply a being, but the being that is most of all. Still another way in which truth grounds itself is the essential sacrifice. Still another way in which truth becomes is the thinker's question, which, as the thinking of Being, names Being in its question-worthiness. By contrast, science is not an original happening of truth. (p. 62)

Art, as Heidegger goes on to explain, is an, if not the, "original happening of truth." Hence the title refers, not to the "origin of art" in any causal or commonly historical sense, but to the work of art as origin, as something original. As original as Heidegger's own discussion of art is, this thesis is not itself original, for we have long recognized (at least since Kant, but also in certain statements by Aristotle) the importance of originality in art. Indeed, it is worth recalling this statement from Homer's *Odyssey* in which Telemachus berates his mother for asking the court "minstral" Phemios to refrain from singing about her missing husband:

> Mother, why do you begrudge our own dear minstrel joy of song, wherever his thought may lead? Poets are not to blame, but Zeus who gives what fate he pleases to adventurous men. Here is no reason for reproof: to sing the news of the Greeks! *Men like best a song that rings like morning on the ear.*[2] (italics mine)

Yet, to say that great art (as Heidegger says, "the only kind we are talking about here") is original is one thing; to understand what this originality entails, what it means, is quite another. In order to understand this originality more profoundly, more originally, Heidegger reminds us of the "true meaning," the "etymology," of "origin" (*Ursprung*):

> Art . . . is the spring that leaps to the truth of what is, in the work. To originate something by a leap, to bring something into being from out of the source of its nature in a founding leap—this is what the word *origin* (German *Ursprung*, literally, primal leap) means.

This passage comes from the final pages of Heidegger's essay and, as such, cannot be understood without understanding much of what preceded it. We will thus have to return to the beginning—the origin—of the essay in order to reach this point ourselves. But we can note, at the outset, the relevance of this passage to our attempted (re)interpretation of Heidegger's essay in synaesthetic terms. Something leaps forth in even the most static of artworks, and, as such, the experience of art is synaesthetic. Moreover, what leaps forth in art is its truth, is what happens when art is experienced as art, not as something else, such as its name, its "object," its objective status (genre, period, etc.), its authorship, etc. The essence, the truth of art, is in this leaping forth, this originality. As such, we have reason to suspect that the essence of art, its truth, is a *primal* movement that underlies any movement as such—a movement that synaesthetically "brings together," for example, "word and image *at the origin* of each."[3]

The Origin of the Work of Art is but one of many places where Heidegger grapples with the important philosophical question of thingness. For example, in *What is a Thing?* which appeared the same year as the essay in question, Heidegger discusses how our customary thinking of thingness does not really get at the underlying, "unconditioned" thing that we think we are thinking about. (It is for this reason that the "thing-in-itself" is used to refer to the notoriously problematic, if absolutely necessary, metaphysical "absolute.").

> With our question "What is a thing?" we not only pass over the particular rocks and stones, particular plants and their species, animals and their species, implements and tools, we also pass over whole realms of the inanimate, the animate, and tools, and desire to know only "What is a thing?" In inquiring this way, we seek what makes the thing and not what makes it a stone or wood; what conditions (*be-dingt*) the thing. We do not ask concerning a thing of some species but after the thingness of a thing. For the condition of being a thing, which conditions the thing as a thing, cannot itself again be a thing, i.e. something conditioned. The thingness must be something un-conditioned (*un-bedingtes*). With the question "What is a thing?" we are asking for something unconditioned. *What is a Thing*? (pp. 8–9)

"Un-conditioned," one will recall, is the etymological equivalent of "ab-solute," and, as I have argued elsewhere,[4] the connection between the unconditioned absolute and art, between the "thingness and the thing" and art, had already been made by Kant and his successors in the German Idealist tradition

(Fichte, Schelling, Hegel, Schopenhauer, and others). But, while Heidegger devotes most of *What is a Thing*? to Kant (not, however, to his third *Critique*, which is devoted to art and teleology), it is here, in this treatise on art, that Heidegger will spell out the relation—indeed, the identity—between art and the mysterious "thingness of the thing."

While the artwork is a thing and, moreover, a particularly material thing insofar as its physical "stuff" is often viewed as essential to its very being ("painting," "film," etc.), it also goes beyond this mere thingness in expressing something else, something other. Heidegger refers this "speaking otherwise" to art's symbolic status as "allegory—*allo agoreuein*" (p. 20), but he also insists that this otherness is not separate from its material substance, its "thingness": "Our aim" is to get at the whole work, the "full reality of the work of art," and so "we must first bring to view the thingly element of the work."

The dichotomies that have plagued our understanding of art, such as Hegel's version of the ubiquitous "form/content" duality, "assault" the experience of art, which conjoins form and content, matter (thingness) and idea: "Thus the interpretation of 'thing' by means of matter and form, whether it remains medieval or becomes Kantian-transcendental, has become current and self-evident . . . it is an assault upon the thing-being of the thing" (p. 30). Art, for Heidegger, is a "thing-being" in which matter and form are one. Art thus challenges a form/content dichotomy that undermines the originality of the work of art: "Form and content are the most hackneyed concepts under which anything and everything may be subsumed" (p. 27). As I hope to show, it is Heidegger's aesthetic alternative to the form/content dichotomy, in which the "thingness of the thing" speaks in its own terms, that constitutes the synaesthetic originality of every genuine work of art.

Although he does not invoke Kant's crucial notion of "disinterestedness" as a necessary condition of the practical uselessness of the work of art, Heidegger too defines art in opposition to any ordinary use function. Although tools and, indeed, most "ordinary objects . . . are all grounded in such usefulness" (p. 28), such objects "do not have the character of having taken shape by themselves, like the granite boulder" (p. 29), whereas the artwork is "something produced by the human hand; however, by its self-sufficient presence the work of art is similar rather to the mere thing." As in Kant, the artwork is both a thing "in itself" and a thing that is capable of being known or understood in more practical, objective terms. But if art reveals the thing "in itself," the "thingness of the thing" beyond whatever objective determination we might also give it, how does this experience of the thingness of the thing, rather than of the object as such, happen? How does one experience the origin of the object as such in the artwork, rather than the object as such?

To experience the "thingness of the thing" should be the easiest thing in the world, but it turns out to be the hardest because it is blocked by the very consciousness that can only experience something in terms of an objective definition that destroys the very thing it purports to apprehend. "What seems easier than to let a being be . . . or does this turn out to be the most difficult of tasks . . . the unpretentious thing evades thought most stubbornly" (31). In order to show how the artwork solves this problem, how it reveals the otherwise "easy" thing-in-itself despite its "stubborn self-refusal," Heidegger begins his now-famous ekphrastic description of van Gogh's *Shoes*.

Although Heidegger refers to a number of different works of art in the course of his essay—the Greek temple of Paestum, the Roman Fountain of C.F. Meyer, poems of Hölderlin (of course), etc.—the ekphrastic discussion of the *Shoes* of van Gogh is the longest and has itself led to many later discussions of his discussion. Similar to James' attempt to describe "the origin of the work of art" as the "figure in the carpet" (discussed in Chapter 1), Heidegger too is forced to "double down" on his terms; where, earlier, James had spoken of the "passion of his passion," here Heidegger says how the painting reveals the "equipmental quality of equipment" rather than the equipment—the tools—as such. As in James' doublings, there is a critical difference here between equipment as such and what Heidegger is describing, àpropos van Gogh's painting, as the "equipmental being of the equipment." The "equipmental being of the equipment" is not the mere equipment as such but, rather, the shoes as they exist synaesthetically as part of the world around them:

> The peasant woman wears her shoes in the field. Only here are they what they are. They are all the more genuinely so, the less the peasant woman thinks about the hoes while she is at work, *or looks at them at all*, or is even aware of them. She stands and walks in them. That is how shoes actually

> serve. It is in this process of the use of equipment that we must actually encounter the character of equipment.
>
> As long as we only imagine a pair of shoes in general, *or simply look at the empty, unused shoes as they merely stand there in the picture*, we shall never discover what the equipmental being of the equipment in truth is . . . a pair of peasant shoes and nothing more. (p. 33)

"And yet—" Heidegger thus begins his famous (for some, infamous) description of how van Gogh's painting reveals the "thingness of the thing," the "thing-in-itself," beyond the mere object as such. It is surprising that some have ridiculed the following ekphrasis[5] when it is clear that Heidegger is being perfectly consistent in going beyond the mere object as such:

> From the dark opening of the worn insides of the shoes the toilsome tread of the worker stares forth. In the stiffly rugged heaviness of the shoes there is the accumulated tenacity of her slow trudge through the far-spreading and ever-uniform furrows of the field swept by a raw wind. On the leather lie the dampness and richness of the soil. Under the soles slides the loneliness of the field-path as evening falls. In the shoes vibrates the silent call of the earth, its quiet gift of the ripening grain and its unexplained self-refusal in the fallow desolation of the wintry field. (pp. 33–4)

"The equipmental quality of the equipment indeed consists in its usefulness. But this usefulness itself rests in the abundance of an essential being of the equipment" (p. 34). Heidegger is showing how the painting reveals, not being, but the Being of beings, the "silent call of the earth" that cannot be heard as such. But Heidegger also describes his own description in decidedly synaesthetic terms: "***This painting spoke****. In the vicinity of the work we were suddenly somewhere else than we usually tend to be*" (p. 35). Rather than ridiculing Heidegger's description as naïve by filling van Gogh's *Shoes* with a clichéd "peasant woman" (Heidegger is perhaps guilty of some things, but naiveté in his writings is certainly not one of them), Heidegger uses the figure of the peasant woman and the "toilsome tread of the worker" to reveal the synaesthetic truth of a painting that is "speaking" to us of something other than the mere painting as such. In having the painting speak to us in this obviously fictitious way Heidegger is revealing how the thingness of things appears in a work of art beyond what one is actually looking at. As indicated by my italics, Heidegger often refers to the importance of seeing what we do not see: the peasant woman isn't looking at the shoes in their moment of truth; we cannot "simply look" at the Shoes in order to see them. This is because what we see in a work of art is not what we see but, rather, what we hear in what we see synaesthetically. As Derrida argues in *Memoirs of the Blind*, what we see in a great drawing or painting is precisely what we don't see.

De-con-struction as Syn-aesthesia: *Memoirs of the Blind*

Many of the late French philosopher's writings, and those of the "school" of deconstruction that followed in their wake, are not only compatible with the notion of art as synaesthesia but, I would argue, synonymous with of the idea of art as "always already" existing outside any of its known or perceived boundaries. Moreover, post-structuralist "methodologies" like deconstruction have, I believe, a lot to gain by incorporating synaesthesia into their Nietzschean goal of "reversing Platonism" (Deleuze) and, particularly, Plato's rejection of art in the name of science, for as long as we continue to define art according to artificially objective boundaries, even if we are trying to "deconstruct" those boundaries, we are trapped in the realm of what Schelling referred to as "negative" philosophy. In this work (and elsewhere), Derrida offers many positive statements about art's meaning that become even more concrete when understood as "blindly groping" (one of the main themes of the *Memoirs of the Blind*) toward the "secret," synaesthetic meaning of art.

"Deep down, deep down inside, the eye would be destined not to see but to weep. For at the very moment they veil sight, tears would unveil what is proper to the eye" 126. This statement comes at the end of Derrida's book/essay, a somewhat unusual work in the ever-burgeoning Derridean corpus because it is a large "coffee-table" volume written as a catalogue for an exhibition of drawings at the Louvre, and so containing numerous "master drawings" interspersed throughout the text. Although coming at the end of his book I quote this statement here for two reasons: first, because it happens to use the same phrase that Henry James had used in the story we discussed earlier to describe the secret meaning of art. "Deep Down," we recall, was also the title of

Gwendolyn Erme's last novel, a book written, we are told, under the influence of her having learned the "figure in the carpet." The truth of art is, indeed, "deep down," not because it is overly complicated, like some sort of puzzle, but because it is textured "in the carpet" of another sensory experience just as the "figure" in a Persian carpet is embedded in wool or some other cloth. Second, this passage from the end of Derrida's book also reveals the link to synaesthesia that we will try to demonstrate in focusing on Derrida's discussion of the two origins of painting—the myths of Butades and Medusa—according to which "what is proper to the eye" is not what is seen as such, but "what" is seen through the veil of tears. One does not literally see the master drawings of Rembrandt, Chardin, and others; what one sees when one "sees" a great work of art is revealed—re-veiled—in something other than what is seen as such. Finally, we must recall, in this synaesthetic figure of weeping vision, one of the most famous instances of synaesthesia in poetry, namely, the passage from Dante when Francesca, in telling Dante the story of her particular fall from grace, declares that she will speak "in words of flowing tears" (tr. Musa): *dirò come colui che piange e dice*.

Although any idea of an "origin" is somewhat anathema to deconstruction—and particularly Derridean deconstruction—as incompatible with an "always already" that views any such beginning as the mythic positing of a nonexistent past by an equally nonexistent present, it is still possible to discuss, as Derrida does here, the two *mythic* origins of painting found in Greek literature, the one explicitly about the origin of painting and the other—the myth of Medusa—the story of how a particular painting came to be perhaps the most famous depiction in classical and pre-classical antiquity. Although seemingly opposed as stories about love and horror, this opposition is superficial, because the story of Perseus' decapitation of Medusa can also be viewed—à la Freud and others—as the story of desire for a beautiful woman (for such Medusa was before her transformation by Athena) that turns to hatred, fear, disgust, etc. as a way of repressing desire for that which must be denied as such. What must be denied as such, according to Freud's famous interpretation, is the son's love for the mother or, more specifically, for the mother's "sex," which results in the transformation of the Medusa's hair (which Freud refers to as the "adult genitalia . . . probably that of the mother") into a castrating force that is redoubled in numerous ways: the need not to look at it, the need to repeat the repression by decapitation, etc. The Medusa, in short, is the original manifestation of what Barbara Creed refers to as the "monstrous feminine,"[6] the dreaded woman whose horrific loathsomeness is merely the repression of unacceptable desires—merely, if you will, a powerful form of the familiar "sour grapes" phenomenon of turning something beautiful into something distasteful when it cannot be obtained.

The more appealing love story of Butades can be seen as the same story as that of the Medusa in other ways than both being stories about the origin of painting. (We will follow Derrida and others in calling the young woman who first draws the silhouette of her departed lover "Butades," although it is actually the name of her sculptor father, the one who turns his daughter's memento into a work of art.) Indeed, as the Medusa figure is far more ancient, and hence "original," one can distinguish the two stories as more or less primitive—as, in psychoanalytical terms, more or less repressed and more or less expressions of the Unconscious. Beauty, in Freudian terms, is a more repressed—less unconscious—expression of desire. Hence Freud's statement that "the sight of the genitals," which is what the Medusa represents, is "rarely considered beautiful." Moreover, as Hagi Kanaan has argued,[7] the Butades story, like that of the Medusa, also involves "*eros* and *thanatos*," desire and the destruction of that desire. And, finally, the two stories are united as stories of the blind: Medusa is seen because she cannot be seen, and Butades' "staff [with which she draws her lover] is a staff of the blind" (*Memoirs*, 51) because the painting allows her to see what she cannot see.

In both cases painting is a painting of the blind, understanding the "of" in both senses of "of," as both painting *of* what one cannot see *by* someone who does not see. Derrida's thesis, that the art of drawing is not so much about what one sees as what one does not see is not as controversial as it might appear. The "trait" that with-draws the moment it is drawn, or even seen, leaving only a trace of what it "really" is, is a familiar enough trope or figure of Derrida's thought ("But where have we ever seen that there is the same relation between the sun and its rays as between sowing and the seed?" p. 44[8]). More simply put, one might refer to the experience of looking at a drawing, such as any of the master drawings from the Louvre included in Derrida's volume by Rembrandt,

Chardin, and others—of following the lines of a drawing, which disappear as quickly as they appear, producing an eclipse or ellipse of vision, as it were, in which one always sees what one does not.

A curious blindness, indeed, for it replaces, like the famous *fort/da* game of Freud's nephew, the absent object of desire with one that is more present, more seen, than the original object ever was or could be. Butades' lover, his actual name and face forever lost, is now seen "forever," or at least until 146 B.C., when the tiles made by Butades' father from his daughter's prototype were supposedly destroyed by the Romans with the rest of Carthage. Medusa's unbearable visage likewise became omnipresent, not only in the celebrated showings by Perseus, and in the aegis of Athena, and in the parade shield of Caravaggio on display at the Uffizi in Florence, but up to the present day, as in the emblem of the house of Versace or on the cover of an Annie Lenox album. As Derrida notes: "Each time one wears a mask, each time one shows or draws a mask, one repeats Perseus's heroic [*sic*] deed. . . . *Perseus could become the patron of all portraitists*" 73 (italics mine).

If painting is thus blind because it sees more, not because it sees less, it is because painting returns us to a wholeness that reveals an origin that is more than we can see. It is not the daughter Butades who is the real origin of painting; rather, it is her father, the real "Butades," who transforms his child's sketch into a work of art,[9] thereby transforming the mere "sign" of the lover's presence into a symbol that, like all symbols, reveals what is and is not there. Likewise, if the depiction of the Medusa is the "mother of all painting" it is because it both reveals and hides itself as the image, according to Freud, of a mother's love that is and is not there. These two origins of painting, then, also represent all painting in revealing, or re-veiling (one version of the Butades myth has her tracing her lover's image on a veil, not on a wall) a wholeness that one never sees unless one loses one's customary way of seeing—unless, that is, one "has eyes to see" as opposed to those we normally use to supposedly see.

In a recent documentary about Amy Winehouse the masterful musician insists that she can't write about someone unless she can smell them. In a book about Francis Bacon Nicholas Chare has written that Bacon's paintings are synaesthetic in requiring us to not only see, but also to touch (with our eyes) and smell them.[10] If painting is, as Derrida insists, "of the blind" in both senses of "of," then it is also open to a wholeness that extends to other senses than merely the visual. Butades exists because of an erotic feeling that is, as Kant rightly argued, absent from all art as such. Art, then, is original because it returns us to the origin of things, an origin that we can no longer see as such but that can be experienced in its aesthetic, or better, syn-aesthetic wholeness.

Epilogue: On Friendship as Synaesthesia

". . . als Hören der Stimme des Freundes, den jedes Dasein bei sich trägt." (". . . like hearing the voice of the friend, which every Being brings beside it.") What is the meaning of this strange but simple phrase that Derrida has plucked from the pages of Heidegger's *Sein und Zeit*[11] to include in his own book on *The Politics of Friendship*? What does this little phrase tell us about friendship insofar as it stands in a synaesthetic relation to Being? Derrida elaborates on the context of this phrase about the friendship of Being:

> "Elle (l'écoute) est l'ouverture première et authentique du *Dasein* à son pouvoir-être le plus proper (Das Hören konstituiert sogar die primäre und eigentliche Öffentlichkeit des *Daseins* für sein eigenstes Seinkönnen)." . . . Le *Dasein* n'a une Oreille et ne peut donc écouter que dans la mesure où, "bei sich," il porte l'ami, la voix de l'ami. *Pas d'oreille sans ami. Pas d'ami sans oreille.*
>
> (Hearing is the primary and authentic opening of *Dasein* to its most proper being . . . *Dasein* only has an ear and can only hear to the extent that it carries the friend, the voice of the friend, along with (by) it. *There is no ear without a friend, and there is no friend without the ear.* p. 356; italics mine)

Heidegger's analysis of hearing Being is an important part of his rethinking *Dasein* as separate from but defined—deconstructed, if you will—by our rationally oriented "logocentric" tradition: "When Heidegger argues in *Being and Time* that being-with (*Mitsein*) is constitutive for *Dasein*, he breaks with a tradition that begins its inquiry concerning man by positing an isolated subject."[12] Proper hearing, then, for Heidegger, is precisely what we are *not* doing when, as "isolated subjects," we unsynaesthetically *think* we hear, just as friendship is precisely what we are lacking when, again as thinking subjects, we unsynaesthetically think we know what friendship means.

If a synaesthetic model of Being replaces the non-"acoustic mirror" of specularity[13] with the more convoluted nature of hearing, it necessarily leads to a labyrinthine maze in which, negatively, the usual order of things has been lost but, positively, the return of Being to itself is a-mazing:

> The most astonishing thing *(das Erstaunlichste)* for the Greeks, the thing which provoked the sense of amazement (*thaumâzein*) which Plato speaks of in the *Theatetus* (155d) and Aristotle speaks of in the *Metaphysics* (A2, 982b 12 et suivi), is that beings come together in Being and shine in the light of Being (*What is Philosophy*? quoted in *L'oreille*, p. 375).

The amazement of Being for Heidegger and the Greeks is not something one simply knows, but something to which, according to Heidegger and Derrida who quotes him, we "turn a deaf ear" in simply knowing that "all is one":

> Tout l'étant est dans l'être (*Alles Seiende ist im Sein*). Entendre cela (*Solches zu hören*), voilà qui résonne (*klingt*) de façon triviale, sinon insolente à notre Oreille (*für unser Ohr*). Car personne n'a besoin de se soucier de ce que l'étant appartienne à l'être (*dass das Seiende in das Sein gehört*). Tout le monde le sait bien: l'étant est quelque chose qui est. (*What is Philosophy*? quoted in *L'oreille*, p. 375)
>
> (Every being (*Seiend*) is in Being. To hear that sounds trivial, even offensive to our ear. For no one needs concern him/herself that being belongs in Being. The whole world knows it well; every being is something which is.)

Really knowing—hearing—that "all is one," according to Derrida's reading of Heidegger's reading of Heraclitus's fragment #50 in *What is Philosophy*? is only possible if one is "astonished" to realize that disparate things are synaesthetically "gathered together" (*logos* in its original sense of "gathering" versus "reason"[14]), notwithstanding their difference, just as knowing that the "sun is new every day" (fr. 32) is only possible if one is *astonished* to realize that the same sun is new each day, and not the same one. It is thus that Heidegger refers to the transitivity of "ist," and also why there is a communal, synaesthetic essence ("Das Sein is die Versammlung-*Logos*") with regard to both acts of wisdom which holds together the difference of *seienden* in the unity of *Sein*.

And this is also why Heraclitus says that the "philosophical man *loves* (*philei*) the truth [*to sophon*]," as opposed to *knowing* the truth (or, one might add, knowing that one loves the truth), for this unity-in-difference of *Sein/Dasein* is always a matter of the pleasure—whether of amorous love, or friendship, or of mimetic metaphoricity—which accompanies essentially disparate beings who are synaesthetically one. And, finally, this is also why synaesthetic "Being conceals itself" ("physis krupteshei philei" Heraclitus fr. 123), for the amorous being of friends/lovers, and the amorous Being of beings, and the amorous being of metaphor and figuration in general as the "language of passion" is in an "éclat" where true difference is hidden as soon as it appears.

But what does all this talk about the astonishing Being of beings say about "hearing the voice of the friend?" And, more specifically: Why does Heidegger refer to the synaesthetic *Sammlung/Logos* of Being/*Dasein* as a hearing ("Hearing even constitutes the primary and authentic openness of *Dasein* for its ownmost possibility of being")?

Heidegger frequently complains that ordinary seeing/hearing/knowing blinds us to the truth of Being. But Heidegger also takes great pains to guard against the assumption that what is meant by "correct" seeing and hearing is merely to be understood as something *analogous* to sensory seeing/hearing. Indeed, the very word "analogy" raises Heidegger's hackles insofar as it confuses the logos of Being with reason or "logic" and in the process *forgets*—in the Nietzschean sense of *vergessen* discussed in the preceding chapter—real speaking and hearing: "in the word "correspondence" (*Entsprechung*) we hardly think any more of *sprechen*"[15] (and, we might add with regard to the English terms used here, of "responding" and "speaking"). As we shall see in the following chapter on Baudelairean "*correspondances*," those are profoundly different from their more customary, analogical meaning. What, then, does Heidegger mean by the correct seeing/hearing of *Sein*? by the "gathering gatheredness" of the original meaning of "logos" as Being, of *Dasein* as "another kind of hearing" (B/T 251)?

As Derrida notes (p. 376), and as Heidegger states often enough himself, the poet hears "correctly," just as the painter sees "correctly": "Art is the opening up of the Being of beings."[16] By "correctly" Heidegger means that when the poet says/hears that something "is," when the poet says "*ist*," what is said/heard is not a simple statement of fact, nor (which would be the same thing) simply there for the senses, nor merely a metaphorical/analogical correspondence between the two. The problem, according to Heidegger, with the classic, analogical definition of metaphorical mimesis (beginning with Aristotle) is that it wrongly describes the poet as transposing something sensory "metaphysically" into the abstract realm of thought or vice versa. But if the sensory is never really sensory but already something which is known, and if the known is never really known but already something that is sensory, then it would be wrong to say that metaphor *transfers* (another word for metaphor and so, in itself, hardly literal) what is sensory into the realm of thought. This is not at all what poets and artists do, although it is what is traditionally thought—beginning with Plato and Aristotle—that poets and artists do. What the poet does, as is evident in his/her use of "living" figures versus the sort of "dead" metaphors that Aristotle uses to argue his case for metaphor as analogy, *is to synaesthetically hear what the metaphor sees "is-there" versus what is already seen or heard or thought or known—precisely the original thinking Heidegger is referring to when he describes real thinking synaesthetically: "Das Denken soll Hörbares erblicken" ("Thinking should bring into view something one can hear")*.[17] Correcting Aristotle's classical, analogical notion of metaphor, Heidegger explains that what the poet sees and/or hears is as much about putting something "between the ears" as it is about putting something "before the eyes" (*pro ton ommaton*):

> Cette oreille du poète tient ferme auprès de l'origine dont il a la passion. Le poète est constant dans l'écoute de ce qui advient originairement et proprement (*was da eigentlich geschieht*) et de ce qui en general "est" (*überhaupt "ist"*) (p. 201—Derrida is referring here to Heidegger's reading of Hölderlin's *Der Rhein* in his seminars of 1934–5). (p. 376)
>
> The poet's ear holds firm to the origin for which he/she is passionate. The poet is constant in hearing what happens originally and properly and what in general "is."

Through his/her use of synaesthetic metaphors (there are no other kind) the poet sees/hears what *is there* (the "da" of *Da-Sein*), not what is already known or supposedly perceived by the senses. The poet hears, the painter paints the "*ist*," which is always "synaesthetic" not because it transposes what is heard/seen into what is known but because it hears properly what is known. As noted in the previous chapter, Heidegger argues in his treatise on *The Principle of Reason* (*Der Satz vom Grund*) that the poet hears (or sees) the proper ground of beings, which is concealed from what is ground-ed in thought. This is a reversal of the customary view in that the metaphorical is now the proper, that is, the literal, while the literal is the "metaphorical" insofar as it has ceased to hold onto its relation to the literal/metaphorical. (In our previous discussion of *Truth and Lies . . .* Nietzsche describes this reversal as the same loss of original, synaesthetic thinking.)

It is important to keep this sense of original, poetic thinking in mind whenever one tries to hear Heidegger and understand his sense of *Dasein* as proper hearing (especially given the dearth of references to art in *Sein und Zeit*[18]), and proper hearing as hearing the voice of the friend: the "friend" is, in this sense, the original metaphorical ground of Being in which one discovers the self outside itself, just as a metaphor, like friendship, "gives us two ideas for one" (Samuel Johnson), versus the one-idea-for-two of objective thought. But it is also possible to understand such "original thinking" negatively by listening to what Heidegger has to say about reason (*ratio*) in *Der Satz vom Grund, The Principle of Reason*. The traditional grounding of Being as the "principle of reason" ("Nihil est sine ratio," "Nichts ist ohne wahrum") is very different from the proper hearing of Being that occurs in poetic verses such as Angelius Silesius's "Die Rose ist ohne wahrum," "The rose is without why" (Lecture VI of *The Principle of Reason*). In discussing the "logocentric" tradition in which reasoned "Being comes to be as a grounding," Heidegger notes that reasoned knowing is a seeing (Greek e*idein*) that nonetheless often looks past what is seen or known (*idein*), and in so doing fails to see/know what is known, just as the principle of reason looks past what is in seeing only its object (*seiend*):

> When thinking does not bring into view what is most proper to what is seen, then thinking looks past what lies present before it. The danger that thinking may overlook things is often exacerbated by thinking itself, namely by the fact that thinking too hastily presses forward to a false rationale. Such a pressing forward can be especially detrimental to a discussion of the principle of reason. . , *it is plain as day that the principle "nothing is without*

> *reason" says something about beings and doesn't shed the slightest bit of light on what "reason" means.* (46)

It is for this reason that Heidegger proposes a different way of *hearing* (*Tonart*) the principle of reason:

> We come closer here to what can be brought into view *as soon as we more clearly hear—and keep in our ear*—the principle of reason in that intonation . . . "Nihil *est* sine *ratione*": "Nothing *is* without *reason*." The intonation allows us to hear a unison between the "is" and "reason," *est* and *ratio*. (italics mine)

If it is not altogether clear what Heidegger is proposing here about a different way of hearing, a different *Tonart*, that is because it is a different, synaesthetic way of hearing the unheard but clearly known "principle of reason." The essence of reason is not contained in beings (*seienden*) but in the meaningful sound of words whose meaning is their sound and whose sound is their meaning. (Heidegger's hearing of "Ratio est," then, is to be understood as a sort of non-onomotopoeiac onomotopoiea.) *Hearing is not separate from knowing/seeing*, although the purported grounding of reason would make it appear so by identifying knowing with seeing (*idein*) in the dominant logocentric tradition. Synaesthetic hearing must, then, serve as a sort of destruction of this grounded being (*Destruktion heisst: unser Ohr öffnen*[19]), though the reality is that it is merely returning to Being what is concealed by this grounding, a grounding whose "figurative" status undermines its own basis, its own grounding, its own reason. "The Rose is Without Why" is not about knowing that one does not know why there is a rose, but, rather, about *hearing* that the "rose is," "ratio est."

Finally, what Heidegger is describing as synaesthetic thinking/listening is also what is meant by the process of "close reading," the hermeneutic method of reading "poetic" texts that might better be called "close hearing":

> C'est ainsi que, dans la lecture, il devrait être question d'un rapport avec "ce qui est puisé et conquis à la source [à l'origine]." Dans l'écriture-lecture, on voit s'entr'ouvrir un instant (à chaque insant) la possibilité-nécessité d'un accès à l'originaire, et d'un partage de cet accès.[20]
>
> Thus, in reading it should be a question of a relationship with "what has been drawn from primordial sources [from the origin] with a struggle." In

> reading-writing, we see for an instant (at each instant) the half-opening of the possibility-necessity of an access to the originary, and a sharing of this access.

Indeed, I would argue that much of what Heidegger is saying about *Sein* as Being that is revealed/concealed in its truth (*aletheia*) can be understood in synaesthetic, "literary" terms, even in works which ostensibly, as in *Sein und Zeit*, do not discuss art at all. This is not to say that one can "decode" Heidegger's thought in this way, for we need Heidegger to understand what so-called "close reading" means as much as we may need literary theory to understand what Heidegger means. But if proper hearing is to be understood as "close reading," we can now understand better what the latter means as listening to what the text is saying differently as opposed to bringing to it some prior understanding of what it means, or taking from it some objective truth of what it has now come to mean. This aesthetic logos of Being as true hearing and seeing resembles Kaja Silverman's notion of a more communal, spectatorial truth that is opposed to the I of *my* knowing—a truth more closely related to the communal, synaesthetic truth of friendship, as friendship is more closely related to it.

4

Baudelaire's Poetry of Synaesthetic Correspondences

What would be truly surprising would be to find that sound could not *suggest color, that color could* not *evoke the idea of a melody, and that sounds and colors were* unsuitable *for the translation of ideas. Baudelaire, "Richard Wagner and Tannhauser"*

Just as there are two major forms of synaesthesia, the literal, "neurological," and the metaphorical, "cultural" type, so there are, as often noted in Baudelaire scholarship, two forms of *correspondances*. One is the literal form represented by Baudelaire's poem of the same name and other explicit references scattered throughout his published and unpublished writings; the other is a more general, less literal form in which the poet's entire oeuvre is marked by various types of correspondences (e.g., his curiously self-referential attitude toward E. T. A. Hoffmann, Poe, and Wagner[1]) that insist upon a poetic identity between different things.[2] To argue that *Correspondances* sets the poetic program of the entire collection is perhaps not that unusual.[3] The argument here makes the same claim but in another way, namely, that Baudelaire's entire oeuvre is informed by synaesthetic correspondences as opposed to the more literal form of synaesthesia, and that a very different sort of reading, and of understanding, of Baudelaire's poetics results from distinguishing the two and, in particular, paying more attention to the synaesthetic mélange of sounds, sights, and scents that is found in all the poems, beginning, of course, with the title of the collection itself. These "correspondences" are no mere symbols or allegories in the conventional sense but, rather, "la force d'incarnation de l'image, grâce au frémissement passionnel qui la traverse, et cela au moment même où le 'solitaire pensif' en dévoile le versant intelligible et abstrait."[4]

In this chapter we will examine, alongside Baudelaire's explicit declaration of poetry as synaesthetic correspondences, a number of other *fleurs* in order to demonstrate these two different forms of correspondence and the synaesthetic essence of Baudelaire's poetry in general. While I agree with Charles Minahen's statement that "faced with a mystery as inscrutable as a sphinx, the poet's aesthetic sublimation of his bewilderment conduces to an awe-inspiring illumination of being, a vision of 'choses infinies . . . Qui chantent les transports de l'esprit et des sens,' uplifting and uniting the whole being, mind and body, in the Iyrical rapture of the poem,"[5] the author would, I believe, acknowledge that such concrete examples of synaesthetic correspondences are to be found in all Baudelaire's poetry, beginning with the strange unity between "flowers" and "evil" that defines Baudelaire's famous—and only—book of poems.

Correspondances

Correspondances

La nature est un temple où de vivants piliers
Laissent parfois sortir de confuses paroles
L'homme y passe à travers des forêts de symboles
Qui l'observent avec des regards familiers.

Comme de longs échos qui de loin se confondent
Dans une ténébreuse et profonde unité,
Vaste comme une nuit et comme la clarté,
Les parfums, les couleurs et les sons se répondent.

Il est des parfums frais comme de chairs d'enfants,
Doux comme les hautbois, verts comme les prairies,
—Et d'autres, corrompus, riches et triomphants,

Ayant l'expansion des choses infinies,
Comme l'ambre, le musc, le benjoin et l'encens,
Qui chantent les transports de l'esprit et des sens.

(Nature is a temple where living pillars
Let escape sometimes confused words;
Man traverses it through forests of symbols
That observe him with familiar glances.

Like long echoes that intermingle from afar
In a dark and profound unity,
Vast like the night and like the light,
The perfumes, the colors and the sounds respond.

There are perfumes fresh like the skin of infants
Sweet like oboes, green like prairies,
—And others corrupted, rich and triumphant

That have the expanse of infinite things,
Like ambergris, musk, balsam and incense,
Which sing the ecstasies of the mind and senses.)[6]

To be sure, *Correspondances* is often discussed as one of the primary examples of literal synaesthesia in art. But Baudelaire was not himself a synaesthete, and the poem itself makes clear that the synaesthetic experience he is describing occurs only "sometimes" (*parfois*), and that the "confused words" are not really words but "symbols," whereas all the literature on synaesthesia insists that real synaesthesia occurs consistently and not occasionally, and that the language/object crossover is not "confused" but literal and very specific.[7] The poem, then, is about a kind of synaesthesia that is essential to the poet's "oeuvre" in general, and not only about synaesthesia "proper." This, I would argue, makes the importance of synaesthesia to aesthetics—synaesthetics—even greater, for it is a kind of synaesthesia that is available to all, and not to the roughly 3–4 percent of the population that are thought to be synesthetes. (When I asked one of these synesthetes recently if she would accept the idea that art is synaesthesia "for the rest of us," she readily agreed, although that is not to say that all synaesthetes would share her view.[8])

However transitory, however poetic and, so, nonsynaesthetically synaesthetic Baudelaire's poem may be, there is no question that "*Correspondances*" is often taken as a virtual manifesto of the synaesthetic experience. The title does not just refer to an abstract unity that one might understand metaphysically as a necessary corollary of the Absolute, wherein everything in art is related to everything else (for this reason, Schelling insisted that there is "really only one work of art"[9]), but it also refers to a kind of epistolary "correspondence" in which, in this case, "*Nature*" is directly addressing—albeit confusedly—the "blessed" individual. "Blessed" because, in the poem that directly precedes this one and, indeed, in its two stanzas immediately preceding "*Correspondances,*" Baudelaire refers to synaesthesia in the language of the Gospels: "Happy is he . . . who can understand without effort the language of flowers and other mute things!" (*Heureux celui qui . . . comprend sans effort/Le langage des fleurs et des choses muettes!*). If the "familiar" message sent by Nature is nonetheless "confused," that is because such absolute "words" are only heard indistinctly, like the "fading echoes" (*longs échos*) described in the second stanza. Words are heard, to be sure, but, like the "secret writing" of Paul Klee discussed in the following chapter, they are signifiers that lack any apparent signification.

The key to understanding the poem's synaesthetic message is to be found in its curious insistence on the "profound unity" between light and dark, and between day and night, that traverses the poem in numerous ways. First, there is the explicit statement that the synaesthetic correspondence between "perfumes, colors, and sounds" occurs "*Dans une ténébreuse et profonde unité,/ Vaste comme la nuit et* comme la claret." More subtly but also more profoundly, there is the alteration between high/bright and low/dark rhymes, which comes to life, as it were, in the final two tercets' stated opposition between certain perfumes that are "fresh as a baby's skin, sweet as an oboe, green as a pasture" and others, "like amber, musk, and incense" that are "corrupt, rich, and triumphant." It is important to include these opposing hues, and even to seemingly privilege, at the end, the darker over the lighter, since such darker associations, such as that of the titular flower with evil, are often deprivileged in society's more moral, valorized understanding. As long as one maintains the day/night, light/dark opposition the synaesthetic vision that Baudelaire is after would be impossible. True poetic synaesthesia must sing in such a way that the literal oppositions framed by that between light and dark vanish in a swirl of truth that underlies our normal comprehension of "des chose muettes."

While there are numerous ways that what we have described as the underlying "primordial substratum" of our synaesthetic potency can be accessed by the nonsynesthete population, many have pointed to the connection between Baudelaire's use of hashish—including the poet himself. It is, of course, well known that the use of certain drugs, such as hashish in Baudelaire's case, can facilitate "psychedelic" synaesthetic correspondences such as the ones the poet is describing here:

> Despite the general consensus that synaesthesia emerges at an early developmental stage and is only rarely acquired during adulthood, the transient induction of synaesthesia with chemical agents has been frequently reported in research on different psychoactive substances.[10]

Among the many interesting results reported in this examination of the numerous studies that have explored the relation between "developmental" (Baron-Cohen) and "drug-induced" synaesthesia is that the latter actually tends to be richer and more complex than the former; that is, the actual synesthete has a more, rather than less, literal connection between the concurrent and its trigger than the nonsynesthete: "Some researchers have emphasized that congenital synaesthesias tend to be relatively simple associations whereas induced synaesthesias are often complex and sometimes reflect inducer-concurrent associations not observed in congenital synaesthesia." In this respect, one might argue that while the synesthete experiences things more "naturally" and directly, the "artificial synaesthete" (and, for our purposes, artistic synaesthesia) may actually expand on, rather than limit, our natural, "original" synaesthetic tendencies. And, finally, the authors also note that artificial synaesthetic experiences, even when "drug-induced," are more pronounced in individuals who are more deeply "absorbed" in their experience, and, moreover, "the result that individuals high in absorption are more prone to chemically-induced synaesthesias is notable because absorption is indiscriminable from fantasy-proneness, and the fantasizing component of empathy is elevated among congenital synesthetes." Such proclivities toward "absorption" and "fantasy-proneness" would, again, point to the relation between both forms of synaesthesia ("developmental" and artificial) and art.

In the same collection as Baudelaire's famous declaration of poetic synaesthesia, where "perfumes, colors, and sound correspond," there is another poem that also relies on a number of synaesthetic correspondences:

Les Promesses d'un visage

J'aime, ô pâle beauté, tes sourcils surbaissés,
D'où semblent couler des ténèbres;
Tes yeux, quoique très-noirs, m'inspirent des pensers
Qui ne sont pas du tout funèbres.
Tes yeux, qui sont d'accord avec tes noirs cheveux,
Avec ta crinière élastique,
Tes yeux, languissamment, me disent: «Si tu veux,
Amant de la muse plastique,
Suivre l'espoir qu'en toi nous avons excité,
Et tous les goûts que tu professes,
Tu pourras constater notre véracité
Depuis le nombril jusqu'aux fesses;
Tu trouveras au bout de deux beaux seins bien lourds,
Deux larges médailles de bronze,
Et sous un ventre uni, doux comme du velours,
Bistré comme la peau d'un bonze,
Une riche toison qui, vraiment, est la soeur
De cette énorme chevelure,
Souple et frisée, et qui t'égale en épaisseur,
Nuit sans étoiles, Nuit obscure!»

What a pair of eyes can promise

I love, pale one, your lifted eyebrows bridging
Twin darknesses of flowing depth.
But however deep they are, they carry me
Another way than that of death.
Your eyes, doubly echoing your hair's darkness
—That leaping, running mane—Your eyes,
though languidly, instruct me : "Poet
And connoisseur of love made plain,

If you desire fulfilment of the promise,
The ecstasy that is your trade,
You can confirm the truth, from thigh to navel
Of all that we have said

You will find my white breast heavy
With the weight of their rough, bronze coins

And, under a soft as velvet, rounded belly,
Poised between ambered loins,

A fleece, not golden, but for richness sister
To that hair with darkness bright
Supple and springing and as boundless
As a deep starless night!"

The English title is by David Paul, whose translation (despite the usual misgivings, it is much better than most) also appears here. It is misleading in replacing the original plural with a singular "promise," and the face or, better, look (*visage*) with eyes because, first, the shift from Baudelaire's plural refers to only one promise, that of the climactic vaginal reference, whereas the poem includes the "two large bronze medals" of Baudelaire's mistress Jeanne Duval's aureolae, to which an entire emphatic line (all stressed syllables except for *de*) is devoted. Moreover, one cannot sanction David Paul's translation of the first line's *surbaissés* as "lifted" when the poet means the exact opposite, nor numerous other matters (e.g., ignoring the poet's ocular anaphora of *tes yeux*), which, as we shall see, interfere with a syn-aesthetic versus aesthetic reading/hearing of the poem.

The synaesthetic, poetic correspondences here are, indeed, numerous. Framing the entire poem is the correspondence between the poet and his mistress, the infamous, dark-haired "lady of the night" Jeanne Duval. The bulk of the poem takes the form of a conversation between the two that is, in reality, the poet talking through his mistress or, more precisely, through her *très-noirs* eyes. It would, however, be incorrect to describe this as merely the poet's projection, for we are to assume that he is listening/looking at Jeanne in the same way that certain "mirror-synesthetes" are capable of feeling/hearing the thoughts of another.[11] The poem, in other words, does not question the confluence of the two, nor does it insist upon it; rather, there is a synaesthetic unity that denies and retains the separation between the two lovers.

Tes yeux/Tes yeux/Tes yeux: the poem's striking anaphora is more than a merely formal device. The eyes "do the talking," but since the talking is not really the eyes', not really Jeanne's, not really the poet's, one could just as easily say the "talking does the eyes," the point being that the titular "promises of a look" engages the poet in a total immersion that engulfs everyone and everything in the final "Nuit sans étoiles/Nuit obscure." This is why Baudelaire insists upon the unity between the "enormous" dark hair of his mistress and the pubic hair of her vagina. Despite its obvious shock value, the reader must avoid reading too much into the vaginal reference (a mistake that is facilitated by the abovementioned mistranslation of the plural "Les Promesses" as singular), because to do so is to miss the dark unity that is the poem's real message, which is the synaesthetic correspondence (*Tes yeux, qui* sont d'accord *avec tes noirs cheveux*) of his voice, with that of the look of his mistress, and all that that entails.

It is striking that in a poem where there is so much confusion as to who is speaking, and which concludes with "Nuit sans étoiles, Nuit obscure!" "truth" should be referenced, not once, but twice: "Tu pourras constater notre véracité" ("You can confirm the truth") with regard to the correspondence between the eyes (spiritual) and the lower body (carnal), and "Une riche toison qui, vraiment, est la soeur" ("A rich fleece which is the sister . . .") with regard to the correspondence between the "carpet and the drapes," as they say. Yet it is precisely the oddity of referring to these synaesthetic, poetic correspondences as the truth that is the truth of Baudelaire's poem. This truth is not the traditional one that is defined by the rational consistency of subject and predicate, which also relies on a correspondence but one that is based upon the "law of identity." Rather, this truth insists upon poetic correspondences that would be denied by a more rational truth that would separate the very things that the poem brings together. Baudelaire is speaking, but so is Jeanne Duval, and so are her eyes. The eyes are speaking, but so is her hair (*Tes yeux, qui sont d'accord avec tes noirs cheveux*), and so is her vagina, "qui, vraiment, est la soeur/De cette énorme chevelure." As we discussed earlier with regard to the theory of metaphor in Nietzsche's "Truth and Lies . . .," there are two truths here, one logical and one metaphoric, but there is no question which truth Baudelaire prefers, any more than there is a question which of these two truths Nietzsche, or Heidegger, or Derrida, prefer. The eyes, in this case, are not only "the windows to the soul." They are also "windows to the body," and to the synaesthetic correspondences that begin (or end) precisely where the logical, everyday correspondences end (or begin).

Les chats

Les Chats

Les amoureux fervents et les savants austères
Aiment également, dans leur mûre saison,
Les chats puissants et doux, orgueil de la maison,
Qui comme eux sont frileux et comme eux sédentaires.
Amis de la science et de la volupté
Ils cherchent le silence et l'horreur des ténèbres;
L'Erèbe les eût pris pour ses coursiers funèbres,
S'ils pouvaient au servage incliner leur fierté.
Ils prennent en songeant les nobles attitudes
Des grands sphinx allongés au fond des solitudes,
Qui semblent s'endormir dans un rêve sans fin;
Leurs reins féconds sont pleins d'étincelles magiques,
Et des parcelles d'or, ainsi qu'un sable fin,
Etoilent vaguement leurs prunelles mystiques.

—Charles Baudelaire

Cats

Sages austere and fervent lovers both,
In their ripe season, cherish cats, the pride
Of hearths, strong, mild, and to themselves allied
In chilly stealth and sedentary sloth.
Friends both to lust and learning, they frequent
Silence, and love the horror darkness breeds.
Erebus would have chosen them for steeds
To hearses, could their pride to it have bent.
Dreaming, the noble postures they assume
Of sphinxes stretching out into the gloom
That seems to swoon into an endless trance.
Their fertile flanks are full of sparks that tingle,
And particles of gold, like grains of shingle,
Vaguely be-star their pupils as they glance.[12]

As in the preceding poem, where a woman's "pussy" replaced the notion of heaven, so here the "Cats," whose infernal properties are explicitly addressed in the poem, have replaced the divine in a Baudelairean world of carnal, poetic correspondences. Also like the preceding poem, which ended between his beloved mistress's legs, here too the final stanza refers to the cats' "fertile loins" (*reins féconds*), where "magic sparks abound" (*sont plein d'étincelles magiques*). Unlike the preceding poem, however, the stars that were noticeably absent ("Nuit sans étoiles") in the final line are here present, figuratively at least, in this poem's final line: *Étoilent vaguement leurs prunelles mystiques*. The numerous correspondences *between* these two poems, as we shall see, are matched by the numerous correspondences *within* this poem, where "the cats" are not "anthropomorphized" but, rather, exist separately as well as in synaesthetic unity with the humans who admire them. (In another poem in the collection, *Le Chat*, Baudelaire states explicitly that, when caressing his "beloved cat": "Je vois ma femme en esprit. Son regard, /Comme le tien, amiable bête.")

The obvious question that one must begin by asking, the question which is so obvious that it has often been overlooked by the countless studies of this famous poem (led, of course, by Jakobson and Lévi-Strauss' canonical, if tortured, structuralist essay), is not "Qui parle?" for that is surely the poet, but, rather, "De qui parle?" Whom is the poem really about? Aside from the general observation of "Baudelaire's personal identification with feline qualities,"[13] there are a number of specific points of confusion regarding this question, and this relationship. The comparison of the cats to "lovers and scholars," "lovers of knowledge and voluptuousness," refers, certainly, to the poet himself as well as to these two groups of people; indeed, we have just seen, in *Les Promesses* . . . , the same conflation of knowledge and carnal desires as it applies to the poet and the poet only. But a different sort of identification takes over when, in the second quatrain, the poet declares that these "Amis de la science et de la volupté" "seek out silence and the terrors of darkness." Cats do not really—and I assume they have not changed in this regard since the middle of the nineteenth century—"seek out silence," although the acuteness of their hearing is not in doubt. Nor do they really seek out "the horror of darkness," although their predilection for nighttime is not in doubt, but merely its "terrors." Jakobson and Lévi-Strauss point to the curiously ambiguous nature of the following two lines about Erebus that form a kind of "hinge" in the exact middle of the poem, but their structuralist zeal has caused them to overlook the fact that the real ambiguity occurs a line earlier, where the poet, who is supposedly continuing his comparison to "lovers and scholars," is actually comparing the cats to neither, nor even to themselves. The comparison that Baudelaire is making is to himself, and since it is not really a comparison when the poet's own characteristics have taken over even those of *les chats* themselves, we should, instead, call this a synaesthetic correspondence in which Baudelaire becomes the cats, and vice versa.

A similar problem occurs in the third stanza, where Baudelaire refers to the "grands sphinx allongés au fond des solitudes." Notwithstanding the problem of referring to plural "Great sphinx" when there is only one, if Baudelaire is referring to the "Great Sphinx" of Giza, the reference to these "guardian spirits" existing in isolation (*au fond des solitudes*) is strange, and strained, compared to other, more telling comparisons (e.g., cats as curious, cats as soft and powerful, cats as obstinate, etc.). On the other hand, the attribution makes perfect sense when applied to the poet, and not the cats—a poet whose love of solitude, and strong sense of isolation even amidst a crowd, is infamous. What both of these "problems" reveal, then, is that this poem about "Cats" is not really about cats but, rather, about synaesthetic correspondences between the poet and the cats "inside his brain":

Dan ma cervelle se promène
Ainsi qu'en son appartement
Un beau chat, fort, doux et charmant . . .
Quand mes yeux, vers ce chat que j'aime
Tirés comme par un aimant,
Se retournent docilement
Et que *je regarde en moi-même*
Je vois avec étonnement
Le feu de ses prunelles pâles,
Clairs fanaux, vivantes opales,
Qui me contemplent fixement.

(In my brain there walks about,
As though he were in his own home,
A lovely cat, strong, sweet, charming . . .

When my gaze, drawn as by a magnet,
Turns in a docile way
Toward that cat whom I love,
And when I look within myself,
I see with amazement
The fire of his pale pupils,
Clear signal-lights, living opals,
That contemplate me fixedly.)[14]

If the poem is not really about cats, then, but about the poet/cat, then it is also not really about lovers and scholars, although these are both roles Baudelaire would easily identify with. Nor is it about the cats' noted obstinacy, but about the poet's obstinate devotion to his craft, to his mistress, to his profligate lifestyle, etc. And, finally, this synaesthetic reading helps us to understand the strange final stanza, where the "magic sparks" within the cats' "fertile loins" correspond to their "mystic eyes" (*prunelles mystiques*). In the other cat poem just quoted, the poet sees "with astonishment" the "fire" of his cat's eyes looking at him from within himself, thus signaling a relationship that is not the normal one—even for a poet—between subject and object but, rather, between a subject who sees an object that is a subject within himself, making him an object. In other words, this is a synaesthetic relation in which a second, inner subject/object relationship replaces the first. In this poem the cats' eyes effectively replace the cats' thighs and vice versa; the magic sparks of their eyes are mirrored in the magic sparks of their thighs, which only makes sense synaesthetically as the poet's own internal correspondences with both.

The Scent of a Poem

Surely no poet is more attuned to the poetry of perfumes, or the perfume of poetry, than is Baudelaire. Indeed, one would be hard-pressed to single out certain "perfumed poems" from the rest, so, as a compromise, I have chosen a few of these deeply scented works to demonstrate their synaesthetic "essence" (or perfume) and, by extrapolation, that of all Baudelaire's works and, by extension, all modern poetry given the widely acknowledged enormity of Baudelaire's influence. Again, while *Correspondences* is often cited as revealing the poet's overt interest in synaesthesia, this is misleading; speaking of one of these "perfumed poems" Mario Richter notes:

> Ce "sonnet," étroitement lié . . . à Correspondances . . . montre que la Beauté reside surtout dans la realization de l'unité que la creation dualiste a brisée.[15]
>
> (This sonnet (*Parfum Exotique*) is strictly one with Correspondances in showing that beauty resides, above all, in an original unity broken by our dualisms.)

The poems I have chosen to analyze in this regard succeed one another in Baudelaire's original arrangement of *Les Fleurs*. They are: *Hymn to Beauty*, *Exotic Perfume*, and *Her Hair*. But, in the spirit of a certain synaesthetic contempt for order often invoked by the poet himself, I will begin in medias res, as it were, with the poem most explicitly addressed to a certain *parfumerie*.

Parfum Exotique

Quand, les deux yeux fermés, en un soir chaud d'automne,
Je respire l'odeur de ton sein chaleureux,
Je vois se dérouler des rivages heureux
Qu'éblouissent les feux d'un soleil monotone;
Une île paresseuse où la nature donne
Des arbres singuliers et des fruits savoureux;
Des hommes dont le corps est mince et vigoureux,
Et des femmes dont l'oeil par sa franchise étonne.
Guidé par ton odeur vers de charmants climats,
Je vois un port rempli de voiles et de mâts
Encor tout fatigués par la vague marine,
Pendant que le parfum des verts tamariniers,
Qui circule dans l'air et m'enfle la narine,
Se mêle dans mon âme au chant des mariniers.

(When, with both my eyes closed, on a hot autumn night,
I inhale the fragrance of your warm breast
I see happy shores spread out before me,
On which shines a dazzling and monotonous sun;
A lazy isle to which nature has given

Singular trees, savory fruits,
Men with bodies vigorous and slender,
And women in whose eyes shines a startling candor.
Guided by your fragrance to these charming countries,
I see a port filled with sails and rigging
Still utterly wearied by the waves of the sea,
While the perfume of the green tamarinds,
That permeates the air, and elates my nostrils,
Is mingled in my soul with the sailors' chanteys.)[16]

The rhythm of *Parfum Exotique* is intriguing. Largely abandoning the mechanics of the Alexandrine, the reader is obliged throughout to replace the usual iambs with numerous anapestic triplets (^ ^ ---------, ^ ^ ---------, . . .): for example, not *de tón/ sein chál/eureúx*, but *de ton séin/ chaleureúx*. The prosody of the poem thus enacts the very transport (another word for metaphor) that the poet describes as he is gently wafted away to a tropic isle by the scent of his lover's warm body.

Also eschewing the hegemony of actual sight, the poet closes his eyes to allow his lover's scent to take the lead. As many postmodern critics of our "logo-centric" tradition have noted, our culture, rightly or wrongly, has allowed the visual to dominate the other senses with the result that not only these other "scents-es," but also their potential synaesthetic comminglings are forbidden. Indeed, the "evil" of the titular "Fleurs du mal" is really no more than this revolt against the usual order of things, a revolt that is even greater for challenging an internal, as opposed to merely an external, hierarchy.

Given the poem's repeated emphasis on warmth ("chaud," "chaleureux"), not only in the first two lines but also in the tropical reverie they inspire, one is struck by the poet's decision to ground his reverie in "un soir chaud d'automne." But on further reflection it becomes obvious why. Summer would be redundant, while winter would stifle the possibility of a fantasy that is made possible by the hint of warmth that such a warm autumnal evening provides. In synesthetic terms, autumn is the "trigger" for a corresponding response that is realized by the native warmth of his dark-skinned lover.

Whereas, in Baudelaire's most famous poem of synesthetic correspondences, "nature" was seen/heard/smelled as a "temple" of "living columns," here, prompted by his lover's "parfum exotique," it is "savory fruits," as opposed to "murmured words" ("paroles confuses") uttered by the island's "strange trees." It might be an overstatement to hear "paresseuse" as a muted reference to Paris, the actual location of the poet's reverie, but the crucial distension of its origin and, thus, performance of its lazy dreaminess is a reminder of what Freud says in his essay on "The Poet and Daydreaming"[17] about the return of our repressed, infantile playfulness. Indeed, key to any understanding of this and Baudelaire's other synaesthetic poems is the idea, often mentioned in this work, that synaesthesia originates in our original state of "primary narcissism" in which, among other things, we exist in a state of omnipotent, undifferentiated oneness. And so it is no surprise when the "laziness" of the poet's reverie turns to sexual thoughts in which native women give themselves freely: although "donner" is not stated, it is implied in the final line of the stanza, where "*dont*" and "*étonne*" merge.

The third stanza involves the most jarring synaesthetic correspondence: "Guided by your scent toward charming climates/I see a port filled with sails and masts/too tired to sail again." The clash of metaphor against metonymy here is a reminder of the inherent link between figuration and synaesthesia; perfume elicits both similarities (the various tropical odors, fruits, bodies) as well as, here, the metonymic association with boats in a harbor. Despite attempts to oppose these two "poles" of poetics (leading Jakobson, for example, to famously compare them to the supposed opposition between poetry and prose, lyric and epic, etc.[18]), what unites the two is precisely unity, the primordial "oneness" from which synaesthesia and poetics emerge and return, metaphorically and metonymically.

As if to emphasize even more this commingling of the senses, the final stanza adds that this *vision* of boats in the harbor is accompanied (*pendant que)* by the island's tamarind *scent* (*parfum*) as well as by the *sound* of the mariners' song: "Le sens de l'odorat . . . s'élargit jusqu'à inclure le sens de l'ouïe ("le chant des mariniers").[19] If eyes are no longer the "windows to the soul," this explains the rather strange, and untranslatable pun of "narine" with marine" (or mariners). For it is the nose, or more precisely the "nostrils," that lead directly to the poet's reverie, and to poetry itself.

Chevelure

Ô toison, moutonnant jusque sur l'encolure!
Ô boucles! Ô parfum chargé de nonchaloir!
Extase! Pour peupler ce soir l'alcôve obscure
Des souvenirs dormant dans cette chevelure,
Je la veux agiter dans l'air comme un mouchoir!
La langoureuse Asie et la brûlante Afrique,
Tout un monde lointain, absent, presque défunt,
Vit dans tes profondeurs, forêt aromatique!
Comme d'autres esprits voguent sur la musique,
Le mien, ô mon amour! nage sur ton parfum.
J'irai là-bas où l'arbre et l'homme, pleins de sève,
Se pâment longuement sous l'ardeur des climats;
Fortes tresses, soyez la houle qui m'enlève!
Tu contiens, mer d'ébène, un éblouissant rêve
De voiles, de rameurs, de flammes et de mâts:
Un port retentissant où mon âme peut boire
À grands flots le parfum, le son et la couleur
Où les vaisseaux, glissant dans l'or et dans la moire
Ouvrent leurs vastes bras pour embrasser la gloire
D'un ciel pur où frémit l'éternelle chaleur.
Je plongerai ma tête amoureuse d'ivresse
Dans ce noir océan où l'autre est enfermé;
Et mon esprit subtil que le roulis caresse
Saura vous retrouver, ô féconde paresse,
Infinis bercements du loisir embaumé!
Cheveux bleus, pavillon de ténèbres tendues
Vous me rendez l'azur du ciel immense et rond;
Sur les bords duvetés de vos mèches tordues
Je m'enivre ardemment des senteurs confondues
De l'huile de coco, du musc et du goudron.
Longtemps! toujours! ma main dans ta crinière lourde
Sèmera le rubis, la perle et le saphir,
Afin qu'à mon désir tu ne sois jamais sourde!
N'es-tu pas l'oasis où je rêve, et la gourde
Où je hume à longs traits le vin du souvenir?

(O shadowy fleece that falls and curls upon those bare
Lithe shoulders! O rich perfume of forgetfulness!
O ecstasy! To loose upon the midnight air
The memories asleep in this tumultuous hair,
I long to rake it in my fingers, tress by tress!
Asia the languorous, the burning solitude
Of Africa—a whole world, distant, all but dead—
Survives in thy profundities, O odorous wood!
My soul, as other souls put forth on the deep flood
Of music, sails away upon thy scent instead.
There where the sap of life mounts hot in man and tree,
And lush desire untamed swoons in the torrid zone,
Undulant tresses, wild strong waves, oh, carry me!
Dream, like a dazzling sun, from out this ebony sea
Rises; and sails and banks of rowers propel me on.
All the confusion, all the mingled colors, cries,
Smells of a busy port, upon my senses beat;
Where smoothly on the golden streakèd ripples flies
The barque, its arms outspread to gather in the skies,
Against whose glory trembles the unabating heat.
In this black ocean where the primal ocean roars,
Drunken, in love with drunkenness, I plunge and drown;
Over my dubious spirit the rolling tide outpours
Its peace—oh, fruitful indolence, upon thy shores,
Cradled in languor, let me drift and lay me down!
Blue hair, darkness made palpable, like the big tent
Of desert sky all glittering with many a star
Thou coverest me—oh, I am drugged as with the blent
Effluvia of a sleeping caravan, the scent
Of coco oil impregnated with musk and tar.
Fear not! Upon this savage mane for ever thy lord
Will sow pearls, sapphires, rubies, every stone that gleams,
To keep thee faithful! Art not thou the sycamored
Oasis whither my thoughts journey, and the dark gourd
Whereof I drink in long slow draughts the wine of dreams?)[20]

In many ways the same poem as the last, despite the "trigger" being the lover's hair. What does it matter if the hair triggers the perfume (*forêt aromatique*) as here, or the perfume the reverie—the same reverie, it seems, of an exotic "sun-drenched port" of "dazzling sails?" This poem is another jumble of synaesthetic correspondences, not only the "intra-sensory associations"[21] that, severed from the former, dilute the poem of its sensory mélange.

The excessive number (an even dozen!) of *points d'exclamation*, excessive even for a poet whose use of them is rather commonplace, reflects the greater emphasis on motion here than in the preceding poem just discussed, where the poet and his lover were lying motionless, leading in turn to thoughts of an "isle of indolence" where the harbor was replete with exhausted, motionless sailboats. Indeed, there were no exclamation points in the preceding poem (!), whereas here, beginning with the opening line, the poet and his readers are roused from their slumber with the clarion call *O toison, moutonannt jusque sur l'encolure!/O boucles! O parfum chargé de nonchaloir!/Extase*! And yet there is very little actual movement in the poem. Like the "exclamation *point*" itself, it is the "ecstatic" infinite time of the moment that is filled, not with actual events in "real time," but with the simultaneous juxtapositions of feelings, scents, places, people, and things that are all contained, synaesthetically, in the perfume of the lover's hair. That these synaesthetic correspondences are to be taken literally and not as mere associations is also evidenced by the nonmetaphoric metaphor (or simile) of the "*mouchoir*." A strained comparison, to be sure, but one that is informed by the "rule of thumb" that, rather than mere similitude, such correspondences can also magically invade an otherwise foreign object.

"Langorous Asia" and "burning Africa" are yet other examples of foreign objects and/or places that, despite their opposition, can exist together and simultaneously in the same "object," the "aromatic forest" of the lover's hair. Such impossible contradictions are no mere associations, but rather the kind of impossible identities that also occur involuntarily in "real," neurological synaesthesia. And while the poet "swims in the perfume of her hair" the way that music *lovers*, and/or those with "taste," "sail" on the waves of music, the "*comme*" is less a separation than an identity given Baudelaire's well-known obsession with music as well as his use, here, of identical sailing/water references, all referring back to the "*moutonnant*" of the first line where "waves of hair crash upon the shore of her neckline." The essence of Baudelaire, I would argue, is in making these unexpected connections, where one rides upon "waves of hair" the same way(ve) that one rides upon the waves of (in Baudealire's case) Wagner's music. *It is no mere comparison.*

That a man "full of sap" would "slowly swoon" in the tropical heat is perhaps understandable, but that "a tree and a man" would do so is decidedly strange until one realizes that this is no ordinary "arbre" (are there any in Baudelaire's poetry?) but, rather, the distended equivalent of the man who is merely breathing in his lover's tresses, tresses which, again, are a "wave" upon whose crest the poet is raised. The "ebony sea" of the *chevelure* is not compared to, it IS the "dazzling dream"—not, as translated, merely a "dream"—that, like the plastic words that occur in dreams and in Klee's paintings (Chapter 5), is the thing to which it refers.[22]

Indeed, there follows a complete synaesthetic unity between "la chevelure" and the "resplendent port" where the poet drinks in "le parfum, le son et la couleur," a unity that is "lost in translation" when one treats the reference as separate from the hair that is the real subject of the stanza. The same failure to acknowledge the synaesthetics of the poem also surrenders the connection of the "bras" of the ship (one assumes, those of the oars) to those of the lover who, again, is the real subject of the poem.

"Dans ce noir océan où l'autre est enfermé": the relative clumsiness of this line is in fact necessary, because the lover's hair, into which the poet, "drunk with passion," has plunged, has replaced the lover herself, she who is also submerged under the surface of her hair. Furthermore, both have been replaced by the gentle rocking (*bercements*) of "embalmed leisure" that suffuses the poet's opiated bliss. (The poet's famous obsession with death—also discussed here in the analysis of "Les promesses d'un visage"—may be nothing more than a way to achieve, finally, the synaesthetic unity to which he aspires.)[23]

Cheveux bleus! as we have and will have (Chapter 9, "Joan Mitchell and the Power of Blue") numerous occasions to observe, the color blue is a particular favorite among both synaesthetes and the synesthetically minded. Here, this is not just a way for the poet to refer to the shadows of his lover's dark hair (although that would be significant in and of itself), but to the "azur du ciel" which, midway between the two groups just mentioned, is identical with the lover's hair. Similarly, the "locks twisted with down" that emit a mélange of scents (“coconut, musk, and tar”) mixes various scents and sights that are as exotic as they are mundane.

Longtemps! Toujours! If synaesthesia had a temporal component, it might be this: a “long while” that extends into eternity, for there can be no point of rest when one is dealing with the sort of intoxication (*Je m'enivre*) that is in play here and, indeed, throughout Baudelaire's writings. The “rubies, pearls, and sapphires” the poet imaginatively shakes from his lover's hair are the synaesthetic equivalent of the “coco, musk, and tar” just mentioned; neither is real, but neither can exist without the other. The poet has found his “oasis in the desert,” where he can imbibe the “wine of remembrances.” It would not, then, be excessive!, nor an overstatement!, to say that the “long traits” of imaginary wine are as real as the “long traits” of his lover's hair.

Hymne à la Beauté

Viens-tu du ciel profond ou sors-tu de l'abîme,
O Beauté? ton regard, infernal et divin,
Verse confusément le bienfait et le crime,
Et l'on peut pour cela te comparer au vin.
Tu contiens dans ton oeil le couchant et l'aurore;
Tu répands des parfums comme un soir orageux;
Tes baisers sont un philtre et ta bouche une amphore
Qui font le héros lâche et l'enfant courageux.
Sors-tu du gouffre noir ou descends-tu des astres?
Le Destin charmé suit tes jupons comme un chien;
Tu sèmes au hasard la joie et les désastres,
Et tu gouvernes tout et ne réponds de rien.
Tu marches sur des morts, Beauté, dont tu te moques;
De tes bijoux l'Horreur n'est pas le moins charmant,
Et le Meurtre, parmi tes plus chères breloques,
Sur ton ventre orgueilleux danse amoureusement.
L'éphémère ébloui vole vers toi, chandelle,
Crépite, flambe et dit: Bénissons ce flambeau!
L'amoureux pantelant incliné sur sa belle
A l'air d'un moribond caressant son tombeau.
Que tu viennes du ciel ou de l'enfer, qu'importe,
Ô Beauté! monstre énorme, effrayant, ingénu!

Si ton oeil, ton souris, ton pied, m'ouvrent la porte
D'un Infini que j'aime et n'ai jamais connu?
De Satan ou de Dieu, qu'importe? Ange ou Sirène,
Qu'importe, si tu rends,—fée aux yeux de velours,
Rythme, parfum, lueur, ô mon unique reine!—
L'univers moins hideux et les instants moins lourds?

(Do you come from Heaven or rise from the abyss,
Beauty? Your gaze, divine and infernal,
Pours out confusedly benevolence and crime,
And one may for that, compare you to wine.
You contain in your eyes the sunset and the dawn;
You scatter perfumes like a stormy night;
Your kisses are a philtre, your mouth an amphora,
Which make the hero weak and the child courageous.
Do you come from the stars or rise from the black pit?
Destiny, bewitched, follows your skirts like a dog;
You sow at random joy and disaster,
And you govern all things but answer for nothing.
You walk upon corpses which you mock, O Beauty!
Of your jewels Horror is not the least charming,
And Murder, among your dearest trinkets,
Dances amorously upon your proud belly.
The dazzled moth flies toward you, O candle!
Crepitates, flames and says: "Blessed be this flambeau!"
The panting lover bending o'er his fair one
Looks like a dying man caressing his own tomb,
Whether you come from heaven or from hell, who cares,
O Beauty! Huge, fearful, ingenuous monster!
If your regard, your smile, your foot, open for me
An Infinite I love but have not ever known?
From God or Satan, who cares? Angel or Siren,
Who cares, if you make,—fay with the velvet eyes,
Rhythm, perfume, glimmer; my one and only queen!
The world less hideous, the minutes less leaden?)[24]

Although occurring immediately before the two poems just discussed, I have left this, the more famous of the group, for last, for it will serve as an example of how, even when the poet is discussing more abstract matters (beauty) than more concrete ones[25] (perfume, hair), the poem's synaesthetic properties are still plainly evident.

Let us begin by disabusing ourselves of a common reading of the poem's famous first line: "Do you come from heaven or Hell, oh Beauty?" Like the titular "Fleurs du mal," this is a synaesthetic oxymoron, not the traditional moral quandary of "love gone wrong," or any of the other commonplaces about a choice between virtue or vice. Rather, the poet is again expressing a synaesthetic vision of *oneness* in which beauty is soil-ed, sinful, torturous, and destructive *at the same time* as it is "heavenly." The same look (*regard*) is "infernal et divin," murderous and beneficent—as opposed to commonplaces like that of the "femme fatale," the notion that love can lead to damnation, as opposed to being it.

"Dawn and dusk," a true doubling of unity and difference, are both contained in this look, as is the ominous perfume of an evening storm. And although one might read the "intoxicating kisses" that make the brave cowards and the coward brave as separate from the preceding lines, it is better, because more potent, to say that the lover's glance, her perfume, and her kisses are all part of a synaesthetic unity that straddles its own sensory oppositions as well as the more moral ones.

If, in the next stanza, the poet repeats the initial question of whether beauty "ascends from the abyss or descends from the stars," this is his way of insisting that this is no banal moral dilemma but, rather, an impossible unity that one can never comprehend, which "ne répond de rien." And, while most translators may be forgiven for the difficulty in rendering the notion that "Murder amorously dances on your proud stomach," replacing *ventre* with the more ideal "breast" effaces the poem's dark sensuality and synaesthetic unity between birth and death, beauty and horror.

"Blessed is the flame in which we burn like moths," and, if the poet's logic is sound, "Blessed is the tomb that, dying, we caress in one final act of lovemaking." If one were to invoke the famous *Liebestod* so admired by Baudelaire, one would also have to admit that, in Baudelaire's mind, this is less of an abstraction than a scented reality. Similarly, the "Infinite" into which the lover's "eye, its smile, its feet" all lead the way is preceded by the infinite unity of all these "parts" of a beauty that can only be fetishized, but never realized in their entirety.

In the momentous final stanza, the synaesthetics of beauty, an amalgam of heaven and hell, Satan and God, angel and siren, is realized concretely in the wonderful "yeux de velours," as well as in the "rhythm, perfume, and luster" of a profound truth that is neither heaven nor hell, but both.

5

Plastic Fantastic: Paul Klee's Synaesthetic Word-Images

That Paul Klee radically challenged the traditional, and even the not-so-traditional, relationship between word and image in modern painting has been noted by many of Klee's critics, including Michel Foucault:

> What is essential [in painting from the fifteenth to the twentieth century] is that verbal signs and visual representations are never given at once. An order always hierarchizes them, running from the figure to discourse or from discourse to the figure. This is the principle whose sovereignty Klee abolished.[1]

Fundamental to this challenge to the relationship between word and image is Klee's notion of the *originary*, an important, recurrent term among the painter and his critics:

> Painting and the work of art are originary events: painting enacts and exposes us to the undercurrent of surging energy and force in the arising to presence of nature and life, the movement behind the objective presence of "men, animals, plants, stone and earth, fire water, and air, and, at the same time for all circling forces." In short, painting is for Klee the enactment of energy and force underneath all existence. This is why for Klee "Art does not reproduce the visible; it makes visible." Moreover, as he points out in his lecture *On Modem Art*, the issue is to learn to see, to experience this dynamic movement.[2]

One can add to this phenomenological description of the "enactment of energy and force underneath all existence" that occurs not only in Klee's work but, indeed, in all great art, by examining how and why script—letters and numbers—plays such a prominent role in Klee's oeuvre. If, as we have noted, "word and image come together at the origin of both" in many of Klee's paintings,[3] what does this say about the *word*, about the *image*, and, perhaps most importantly, about their *origin*? Or, again: If art as "an origin, is calling into being something hitherto unseen,"[4] then why include script—which can be defined as always already "hitherto seen"—in an original artwork unless that letter or number is, like the artwork it is a part of, also original, also "hitherto unseen?"

Although Klee was not himself a synaesthete, and although he did not, like his close friend Kandinsky or his "mentor" Robert Delaunay, argue for the synaesthetic significance of his work, his oeuvre is often referred to in the context of synaesthesia.[5] Moreover, the fact that Klee, like Baudelaire, was NOT himself a synaesthete, or even someone who argued for its relevance to his art or art in general, is precisely what will help us to clarify the problematic relationship between art and actual, genetic or "involuntary" synaesthesia.

It is the mere surface of things that allows us to separate words and things in the traditional manner that Foucault described. We speak of things as if they were separate from words, and yet we know that the words "chair," "leaf," etc. are also their objects. That is to say, when we look at the *world* we are also looking at the *words* we use to describe that world, despite the fact that we think we are looking at objects that are separate from their words. So, when Klee famously says that he wants to reveal "the real truth that lies invisible beneath the surface,"[6] and to "make the invisible visible," we can take this to mean that Klee's work reveals, not the wordless thing that we wrongly suppose underlies appearances, but, rather, the word-thing, the *écriture/peinture* that underlies the supposed separation of word and thing that only exists (if it exists at all) on the surface. If, for Klee, "picture and word seem to come together at the origin of each" we can now understand this strange statement as referring to an underlying truth (as opposed to a superficial truth) where the original word/thing exists before it is separated into word and thing, word and image. Fortunately, we have many examples from Klee's oeuvre that show us how this is possible, and what this strange word/thing might look like.

Figure 5.1 "Einst der Grau der Nacht . . ." (1916).

"Einst der Grau der Nacht . . ." (1916) is one of a number of relatively early poem-paintings from the period after Klee's "conversion" to both color and pure abstraction. (We will subsequently examine later works where language evolved—or devolved—into isolated letters and, finally, into writerly marks that resemble letters from an unknown alphabet.) There is some confusion regarding the poem's authorship, but whether it is Klee's own (he wrote many poems) or not, the painterly potential of the poem is evident in, for example, the poem's modulation from *Grau* (grey) to *Blau* (blue) that is represented, in the painting, by the marked division between the upper "grey" half of the work and the decidedly lighter "blue" half of the painting. With this division in mind the poem reads:

Once out of the grey
of night
plunged forth
then heavy
and rich
and strong
from the fire
Evening
Full of God
And bowed
————————
Now aetherly
By the blue
Showered
Hanging
Over the mountaintops
To
Intelligent stars

Some further preliminary observations: first, each letter, for the most part, is drawn the same way; for example, "N" is consistently drawn as two colored right triangles. Second, a correction is still evident in the third line of the second "stanza," where "umschwert" is moved closer to the center than its predecessor. Third, while there are no such lines in the upper part of the painting/poem, the lower half includes two "empty" lines of colored blocks with no letters, one between the aforementioned "Showered" and "Hanging," the other at the end of the poem—there is no such blank line at the beginning of the poem to create a symmetrical "border" with this.

Those familiar with Klee's works will immediately recognize the "Delaunay-esque" pattern of colored blocks or, one might say, "cubes" as the influence of Picasso is also readily apparent in the works of both these painters. It is thus altogether possible to appreciate the watercolor without taking into account the almost indiscernible letters in the way that one can appreciate similar paintings of this period by Klee that do not "illustrate" a poem or, for that matter, contain any words or letters at all.

"Illustrate": In what sense can one say that the painting illustrates the poem? Recalling what was said about the two halves of the painting enacting, as it were, the poem's movement from grey to blue, with the lower half of the painting, with a much greater number of lighter blue cubes, being considerably lighter than the top, one would have to say that the painting does, indeed, "il-lustrate" the poem in the original sense of "giving light to something." If one pictures this painting as a sort of stained glass window then one understands how the light that is transmitted through the cubes illuminates—illustrates—not only the whole poem but every word, every letter, for it is not just the signified but also the signifier that is being illustrated here (which is how this differs from traditional notions of illustration that do not merge the text with the painting).

As is the case with synaesthetes who see certain letters as consistently corresponding to certain colors, the letter "A" is consistently yellow, although one cannot say the same for other letters. This demonstrates what I would call the "semi-synaesthetic" quality of Klee's works: while not synaesthetic in the literal or "genetic" sense, this painting, like all art, is semi-synaesthetic in crossing over from one sense to another. In this case, letters and words and, here, an entire poem are colors, colors that can correspond to specific letters ("A"), words ("*Feuer*"), or ideas (the blue light of the lower half, the row of "stars" in the bottom row), but that can also have a meaning all their own. This last notion is particularly important, because if, in Klee's paintings word and image (or here, color) are one, then the word cannot take precedence over the image any more than the color can take precedence over the word. As in real synaesthesia, the logical separation between the different sense is superseded by a preexistent unity—as Klee himself says, "the great manifold in a single word!"[7]

The next work is one among many in Klee's oeuvre that feature a single letter. We bypass the lexical level of the "word" because those paintings and drawings are not as significant, either quantitatively and qualitatively, in Klee's oeuvre (unlike their frequent appearance among the cubists). Perhaps this is because the word, unlike an entire poem (as in the example just discussed) or the late examples of "unknown script" to be discussed next, forces a certain signification upon us, whereas Klee's use of signs—including his famous use of arrows—avoids the signified in lieu of the signifier, denotation in lieu of connotation.

Figure 5.2 Villa R, 1919.

At the risk, again, of appearing childish, we begin with the obvious question of why there is a large letter dominating the foreground of a supposedly letter-less landscape. The answer, it turns out, is as simple as the question: Why not? Where is it *written* that a landscape must be "mute," must be language-less? The letter "R" is there because it is part of the landscape, just as language is actually part of the "natural" world we see despite, again, a traditional view that would naively separate the two. That is why the commentators are correct in referring Klee's use of script to works outside our classical tradition—Egyptian, Arabic, medieval, etc.—, and why they are also correct in referring such works to a kind of primitivism. But this is not to diminish Klee's originality and, particularly, his originality in such paintings as this, for to deny the false separation between word and thing—word and image—is as revolutionary as Freud's discovery of an unconscious that, while always there, had also always been denied.

In mentioning Freud we are reminded of his numerous statements to the effect that, when words appear in dreams they are not really words but pure plastic signifiers. Dream images, for example, can be "linked together merely through a similarity in the sound of words,"[8] that is to say, a word can be connected to an image through its "signifier" (its material substance) rather than through its "signified" (its logical idea) in much the same way that a real synaesthete connects images through a similar conjunction of signifiers—for example, when a synaesthete associates a particular number with a particular color. (In studies of this particular type of synaesthesia it has been found that the connection is not based on the idea—the signified—of the number but rather by its material shape.[9]) Similarly, in dreams, as in Klee's paintings, "word and image come together at the origin of each" insofar as the word is not separate from its abstract signified but one with it.[10]

Rather than being governed by the logocentric separation between word (signifier) and its image or idea (signified)—a move that Hegel, not surprisingly, praised as the triumph of logical consciousness[11]—in dreams language is governed by what Jakobson famously referred to[12] as the two cardinal principles of poetic discourse, metaphor and metonymy, and which Freud refers to as the two cardinal principles of dream discourse, "condensation" (*Verdichtung*) and "displacement" (*Verschiebung*): "In the process of transforming the latent thoughts into the manifest content of a dream we have found two factors at work: dream-condensation and dream-displacement" (p. 326). If metaphor is inherently synaesthetic in crossing over from one image to another "to which [the first] does not properly belong" (Aristotle), then the first of the two principles governing dreams brings back together—"condenses"—meanings that are no longer logically disparate, exactly as does a genuine, poetic metaphor. Metonymy, which Freud calls "displacement," is even more synaesthetic in replacing a word's meaning, or signified, not with something like it but, rather, with something that happens before, after, or nearby, as when one refers to having "slept with someone." If one follows Freud in thus defining the language of dreams in poetic, synaesthetic terms, then it would be difficult to avoid the conclusion that the infantile substratum of consciousness—the Unconscious—which is the origin of dreams is also the origin of art as well as the origin of our synaesthetic, and quasi-synaesthetic experiences.

"The direction taken by the displacement usually results in a colorless and abstract expression in the dream-thought being exchanged for a pictorial and concrete one" ("Considerations of Representability," p. 354). The pure plasticity of language in dreams is also what characterizes the pure plasticity of language in Klee's painting: here the letter "R" is inseparable from the other geometric shapes that fill the other objects in the painting, although this begs the question of why the letter should dominate the painting. No one would deny that, however much the painting might stand on its own without the letter "R," or however much the letter "R" can be seen as part of the landscape in its harmonizing with the other colors and shapes of the painting, it stands out from the rest of the painting while, at the same time, blending perfectly with it. *And it is precisely this contradiction that explains the remarkable appearance of script in this and other of Klee's works.* For language is both part of the "natural" world as well as separate from it, and so when script appears in Klee's work, as it often does, this is because, as in dreams or other expressions of the unconscious, words are no longer separate parts of our "conscious" being but, rather, things which are not things and not-things which are things—again, where "word and image come together at the origin of each."

The painting is thus an excellent example of why Klee's paintings are and are not synaesthetic, and why those interested in synaesthesia embrace his works despite knowing that they are not explicitly synaesthetic. For just as senses merge in actual synaesthesia and, in a particularly famous form of the nearly eighty different acknowledged forms of the condition, certain letters consistently evoke certain colors ("color grapheme synaesthesia"), the letter "R" here joins with the landscape at the same time as it is decidedly separate from it. It is as if Klee discovered a particular power, not in the letter as such, but in the letter when it magically appears in a landscape that is supposedly other but, in reality, is not. It is as if Klee returned to the very mystery of language, a mystery that our persistent use of language and customary assumption of its identification with the things it represents (an assumption which is merely the tautology of language reifying language) fails to understand. A failure that is also often true of many "academic" views of language, such as the so-called science of language ("linguistics"), but which is contested by a deeper awareness of the inherent mystery of language, such as Heidegger's, which is doubtless one of the reasons for the latter's acknowledged appreciation of Klee.[13]

The so-called "R," which we have already described as both more and less than an actual letter, is also more and less than an actual "R." It is also the initials of the artist's own name (P + K), and while everything else is fairly proportional in size to a traditional landscape (the house, the path, the sun, etc.), the letter, language in general, and the named self from which these are derived are never proportional to the world to which they belong—the ego, for example, is always disproportionately large, however much one tries to temper its solipsistic tendencies.

While it might be tempting to describe this painting realistically—as a night scene in which the "villa" is illuminated by moonlight, with trees in the foreground, a conspicuous path winding around the house and receding into the distance, etc.—this would be a mistake. The real "meaning" of the painting is in its careful orchestration of colored shapes (the white house, the green letters and half-moon, the yellow moon, the blue and purple cubes and triangles, etc.) that closely resemble the many "contemporary" attempts by Kandinsky, Mondrian, and earlier, Whistler, to make painting into "visual music." Viewed this way, as an "abstract" tonal harmony of shapes and colors, the significance of the letter "R" becomes even clearer. The three green shapes making up the letter, shapes and colors that are repeated elsewhere in the painting, should not be seen as separate from the rest of the painting. Rather, the entire painting is a secret language of colored, harmonic sounds that can be heard and seen as clearly as the "R." In this way, the "R" can be seen as blocking the path under it, as if to say that Klee has found another way than the customary one, one that explodes the traditional separation of language, vision, and sound. For this reason it is useful but, ultimately, unwise to single out Klee's paintings that feature letters or language in general from those that don't, and paintings that feature letters that are not recognizable from those that are, for, as evident here, all Klee's paintings can be seen as a new "painted language."

One must approach the many paintings of Klee from the mid-1930s onward that depict a secret language of indecipherable script with a similar caution. The line separating those works, which openly evoke a kind of language, quickly dissolves into other works of the period (e.g, "Face and Body Equally," "Park near Lu(cerne)," the famous "Paukenspieler," etc.) that, while not so obviously script-like, nonetheless make it clear that these different categories are not really different categories at all. For, while the "words" of Klee's late works are really images, the images of Klee's later works are also really words.

The example we have chosen from many such works (the period in question was Klee's most prolific) is appropriately entitled "Secret Writing" ("Geheimschriftbild").

Figure 5.3 Secret Writing, 1934.

Although the translated title is good as far as it goes, it leaves out the "*—bild*"; better, but certainly clumsier, would be "Secret Image Writing." A more significant "mistranslation" is the number of illustrations of this painting that mistakenly show the painting in reverse—from the back, as it were, with right and left switched. I will assume this was merely a mistake and not a reference to Leonardo's own famous secret writing, or to the story by Balzac which Klee (as well as Picasso) was known to have admired concerning Frenhofer's painting "behind the canvas (this is what another Balzacian artist, Frenhofer, asks of the ideal canvas he dreams of)."[14] Although Barthes' passing reference to Balzac's metastory about art, which bears close comparison with *The Figure in the Carpet* discussed earlier, characterizes it as a typical romantic pursuit of "the All," the story itself describes artistic truth, the "figure in the carpet" behind the canvas in less abstract terms:

> Effects! Effects! They're merely the incidental phenomena of life, not life itself. . . . You don't delve sufficiently into the intimate depths of the form. . . . Neither the painter, nor the poet, nor the sculptor should separate the effect from the cause, since they're inevitably interconnected! . . . What's missing? A trifle, but that trifle is everything. You have the semblance of life, but you aren't expressing its overflowing superabundance, that indefinable something, which may be the soul, hovering like a cloud above the outer husk. . . . She's [the figure in the painting] a silhouette with only one side, she's a cutout likeness, an image that couldn't turn around or shift position. I feel no air between this arm and the field of the picture.[15]

If something extraordinary happens when, as in the preceding painting discussed, a letter emerges from an assemblage of nonlinguistic marks, would not something equally extraordinary occur when the opposite happens, as here? When, that is, an assemblage of linguistic marks (as Klee makes clear not only by his title but also by the playful quotation marks in the upper-left and bottom right corners) reverse this order and turn back into an unknown language? These letters—as, indeed, all letters in Klee's work—are not letters as such, or, if they are, they are letters as they exist at the origin of language. Klee's revolutionary breakthrough was at once very simple and very profound, for it ends the separation of word and image by depicting letters (language) that are also images, thus returning us to nothing less than the very origin of language. If writing such as this reflects Klee's sojourn in North Africa and, in particular, his viewing there of Egyptian hieroglyphics, we must also note that what moved Klee was not the actual language of the Egyptians (who did not refer to their own writing as "sacred writing") but, rather, to writing as intelligible markings that do not make sense, as language that would leave its painterly, signifier-esque essence intact. In this respect, the "scare quotes" in the painting (if that is what they are) do, indeed, refer to language "as such."

As many have noted, the letter "X" is not just one letter among others that appear in Klee's works. Klee had a particular fondness for "X's," although there has been no attempt to explain this particular fascination further. As we know, "X" is not just a letter "among others"; it is sometimes used as a letter that stands for all other letters, as when someone who does not how to write "makes his or her mark" with an "X," and it also frequently stands for some unknown quantity or quality and, perhaps most significantly, to the Kantian "supersensible" or "absolute" "thing-in-itself." And, finally, it stands, literally, for the "X" of the *chi*-asmus, the rhetorical "reversal of reversal" that was seen as the secret "figure in the carpet" of James' tale discussed in the Introduction to this work. These associations are all relevant, but to understand this relevance one must first note the most obvious explanation, that while "O's" are a staple of nature, "X" is an immediate sign of signs, or writing. This is a relative distinction, to be sure, but it is also precisely why, while other letters (in particular M's and W's) appear in this *Gehimschriftbild*, X predominates (there are nine here). For X is the model, the template, for all other letters in this and other of Klee's works because, while purely visual, purely "painterly," it is also purely linguistic, the language of language, as it were.

If all the letters of the *Geheimschriftbild* are thus modeled on "X" in being both painterly and linguistic, this tells us that these "pure signifiers" are all, like X, symbols of the supersensible, of the absolute (again: "the great manifold in a single word!"). The problem with merely labeling these marks as "pure signifiers" is that they do refer to something, to some "signified," we just don't know what that is—it is a "secret." The power of this painting, then, and of those like it, is that it is, indeed, a painting of the absolute, of a meaning which, as Kant insisted, is unknowable but not unthinkable,[16] because it is writing at the same time as it is also purely plastic, purely visual. Klee's fascination, and ours, with such *écritures/peintures* is that they show us the absolute, the "other side of the canvas" of a language that is not language, since it is also absolute, also "X."

If, as Schelling insisted in following out the implications of Kant's third *Critique*, all art is an expression of the absolute "infinite in the finite,"[17] then these letters that are images which are letters necessarily cross over between the two, between the image and the idea. They reveal, in other words, the "figure in the carpet," the synaesthetic origin of language—original language—as that which emerges from the purely visual mark but which has not yet evolved into a particular meaning. This again cautions us that Klee's other, so-called nonlinguistic paintings, paintings whose stated goal is also to reveal this absolute, are no less linguistic than these paintings are "purely" pictorial.

Figure 5.4 Death and Fire, 1940.

It should now be apparent from this synaesthetic reading of Klee that notions such as Clement Greenberg's of "pure" painting devoid of such crossover elements is mistaken if, as we have argued here, such synaesthetic crossover elements Are the very purity that is denied by the separation of painting, or any art form, from every other.[18]

6

Rouault's "True Icons": A Synaesthetic Unveiling of the *Miserere's Veronicas*

In German Idealism, beginning with Kant, one frequently encounters the strange notion of "intellectual intuition." What this notion seems to refer to is a vision that is an *intuitus originarius* as opposed to an *intuitus derivatus*—that is to say, a vision of things as they really are, or as "God" supposedly sees them, as opposed to our ordinary view of things as separated from such "things-in-themselves."

> The difference [between Reason and Understanding] turns on a peculiarity of our [human] understanding relative to our power of judgment in reflecting on things in nature. . . . We must have an underlying idea of a possible understanding different from the human . . . it is at least possible to regard the material world as a mere phenomenon, and to think something which is not a phenomenon, namely a thing-in-itself, as its substrate. *And this we may rest upon a corresponding intellectual intuition, albeit it is not the intuition we possess.*[1] (italics mine)

While it may seem even more foolish to ask how God sees things than it is to raise metaphysical questions about the supersensible "thing-in-itself," a number of philosophers took Kant's idea as directly relevant to art:

> There is but one such activity [that resolves the problem of knowing the thing-in-itself], namely the aesthetic, and every work of art can be conceived only as a product of such activity. . . . We have only to analyze the features of this intuition we have now deduced, in order to discover the intuition itself; and, to judge beforehand, it can be no other than *the intuition of art*.[2] (italics Schelling's)

If these philosophers are right, and the very *raison d'être* of art lies in its genius and concomitant originality in producing what has been produced by "God" as opposed to what one produces with one's own hand, then all art is religious, and not just those artworks that advertise themselves as such. While Clement Greenberg and others would reject religious art proper as a redundancy on these same grounds,[3] one could argue that this "redundancy" is to be understood as indicative of an art that is more, not less, essential. One way to test this thesis is to examine the religious work of Georges Rouault as not only aesthetic but syn-aesthetic; for if God is a synaesthete in returning to the original unity of things, then the vision of things "as God sees them," and of God himself, must be synaesthetic.

* * *

In the largest, most compelling recent work on Rouault[4] that has emerged after the dearth of criticism that resulted from the aforementioned denunciation of the artist by Greenberg and his followers, a number of contributors to this extraordinarily rich volume of essays noted not only the persistence, but also the importance, of the Veronica-motif in Rouault's oeuvre. It is not surprising that the painter was drawn to this particular image—indeed, it would be surprising if he were not. For to paint or draw the Veronica as often as Rouault did is to depict an image of an image that is not merely an image but, as the story goes, the true image—the *vera icon*—of Christ himself. Rouault's Veronicas thus become more than mere images because the image itself is more than a mere image. It is real.

In Rouault's most famous graphic work, the fifty-eight large prints of the *Miserere et Guerre* series that the artist worked on in the 1920s but, for various reasons, was not published until shortly after the Second World War, the Veronica occupies a prominent place. Each of the two parts of the work, and thus also the very last print, ends with Veronicas. Since neither of these prints follows any obvious chronological order (e.g., the first appears after the lithograph of "Doubting Thomas" discussed later in this chapter, the only print in the series that depicts the resurrected Jesus), one must conclude that their appearance as conclusions is thematic: in a book of fifty-eight prints (there were supposed to be more), these prints are "conclusive" because they stand for all of the prints as "true images" of Christianity.

The Veronica functions as an inversion of the many versions of a veiled God, such as the famous image of the veiled Isis as hiding "all that is, and was, and will be" underneath her veil.[5] For, in the case of the Veronica, the veil that had been covering the compassionate woman's face now reveals the face of God on its surface; rather than hiding the face, the veil is, in this case, hidden by the face of Jesus. The importance of this reversal cannot be overstated, for if, as Jean-Luc Nancy has recently argued:

> Christian painting is Christianity—or something of Christianity in painting or as painting—caught up in the process of making painting: pregnant with painting, giving birth to it while also announcing itself in it and as it—and, what's more, announcing itself as the entire stakes and the entire history, still today, of what we call "art" . . . the Christian image, joined with the no less Christian refusal of the image . . . bears all the intensity of the access to the inaccessible divine.[6]

then the Veronica would be the first image to inaugurate what Nancy sees as the capability of revealing—rather than reveiling—the "inaccessible divine," or, in the famous words of Paul Klee, to "make the invisible visible."

Nancy's argument should go a long way in correcting the false but widespread view that Rouault's religious art is somehow out of step with modernity (an argument that is, not coincidentally, also contradicted by one of Rouault's spiritual brothers, the quintessentially modernist Baudelaire). The fact that, especially in the modern world, there is a great deal of very bad religious art is no more relevant to Rouault than the fact that a great deal of what goes by the name of "art" is far removed from the very thing it purports to represent. If all true art is, in its essence, the representation of something divine and, as we are attempting to demonstrate here, syn-aesthetic in its representation of an original aesthetic truth, then Rouault's Veronicas do not just represent God but *are* God. How is this possible?

Anyone who has seen the *Miserere* in its original, loose leaf book form can attest to the work's extraordinary tactile qualities. Although often shown framed, something is lost when the thick, cloth-like Arches paper of these large "etchings"

(Rouault refers to them this way, although he employed a number of different techniques, such as aquatint, lithography, etc.) are put "under glass." This is particularly true of the two Veronicas, although, as just argued, it applies to all the prints insofar as they are all "true icons," all images of Christ(ianity). Moreover, of the fifty-eight prints, the two Veronicas are the only ones (with the exception of the "title pages" that begin the "Miserere" and "Guerre" sections of the suite) with what was to become one of Rouault's trademarks, the thick, multilayered frames that appear in many of the artist's paintings and graphic works[7].

Figure 6.1 Georges Rouault, *Miserere*, pl. 33.

Figure 6.2 Georges Rouault, *Miserere*, pl. 58.

These four "frame prints" are also similar in all being "book-ends": as mentioned, the two Veronicas appear at the end of each part just as the two title pages appear at the beginning of each part. The significance of this, I believe, is the idea of the frame itself: just as the holy face appears on a cloth that reveals rather than "re-veils" the face, so the cloth itself is imbued with the spirit it represents. The cloth IS the image, which IS the holy face, which teaches us that we must not, as we all too often do, separate the work of art from its frame, which, as Kant said, is a distraction unless it enters into the truth of the work of art itself.[8]

There are, of course, many versions of the Veronica, the most famous being the early seventeenth-century version by Domenic Fetti, which was thought to have been influenced by the "actual veil" shown in St. Peter's crossing in 1606 (that veil, that had been in Rome since the twelfth century, disappeared in 1608).

Figure 6.3 *The Veil of Veronica* by Domenico Fetti, 1618.

One might wonder why Rouault's Veronicas show Jesus with eyes closed, as opposed to Fetti's and others', which, as one would expect, portray the still-living Christ with his eyes at least partly open. The answer to this is both simple and intriguing. As a number of essays in the *Mystic Masque* noted, Rouault was profoundly moved by the famous photographs of the Shroud of Turin that became wildly popular in 1898.

Figure 6.4 *The Shroud of Turin.*

In the Turin Shroud the eyes, as one would expect, are closed; this, and the lithographic qualities of the negative that revealed, for the first time, the face with considerably more clarity, as well as the similar placement of the cranial stigmata, have led critics to believe that Rouault modeled his Veronicas on the Shroud, which was thought at the time—and for a long time after—to be genuine. This should not be taken as a mistake on Rouault's part. Rather, because Rouault believed the Shroud to be the "holy face," it should be taken as a sign of Rouault's conviction that in his own Veronicas he was not depicting a mere image but the true image—the *vera* icon—of Christ.

We will address, in a moment, the synaesthetic power of Rouault's two "true images," a power that is heightened more, not less, by its less realistic style than that of the many earlier versions. But first let us consider another form of synaesthesia that has been noted with regard to the Veronicas, and to Rouault's in particular:

> Inevitably, Veronica invites us to consider what it is we see in the image that she holds; she summons us to the gaze of self-reflection as we look on the cloth. "Christ's face itself is very like a *vera* icon, or better, its archetype (but in turn, as part of a pictorial fiction) and is looking to the viewer who becomes the Veronica, and taking the place of the saintly woman, receives the impression of the face in the screen or veil of her/his mind."[9]

What Father Keenan, and Wolf and Schongauer whom he is quoting, are all referring to is, I would argue, a form of synaesthesia in which the miracle of Christ's face's imprint on the cloth is no mere reproduction but the actual face of Jesus, and the "impression" on the viewer's face is no mere impression but the unity of the holy visage with our own, as undeserving as we may be. Similarly, the representation of the "true icon" in a true, original work of art like Rouault's is not meant to be any mere reproduction of the original Veronica but a synaesthetic unity in which, as in all true art, all "vera icons," we become (via the "hermeneutical circle") the "object" we are seeing.

Before turning to the two images themselves, let us also note other important aspects of the Veronica story that may prove relevant to our reading. The story of Veronica is not part of any of the Gospels, but, as Father Keenan (following others) argues, "The legend, like the cloth on which it appears, evolved through history by absorbing one narrative into another" (p. 439). It evolved, first, from a story that *does* appear in three of the Gospels involving the "Hemorrhissa," a woman had been hemorrhaging for twelve years before being miraculously cured by Jesus after she surreptitiously touched his cloak:

> As Jesus was on his way, the crowds almost crushed him. And a woman was there who had been subject to bleeding for twelve years but no one could heal her. She came up behind him and touched the edge of his cloak, and immediately her bleeding stopped. "Who touched me?" Jesus asked. When they all denied it, Peter said, "Master, the people are crowding and pressing against you." But Jesus said, "Someone touched me; I know that power has gone out from me." Then the woman, seeing that she could not go unnoticed, came trembling and fell at his feet. In the presence of all the people, she told why she had touched him and how she had been instantly healed. Then he said to her, "Daughter, your faith has healed you. Go in peace." (Luke 8: 43-48)

The story is imbedded in another one that, according to Keenan, joined with the former in eventually combining to form the Veronica myth. The incident with the Hemorrhissa occurs when Jesus is on his way to save the dying twelve-year-old daughter of Jairus, a high-ranking Jew, whom Jesus had to raise from the dead because he was late arriving to save her, presumably because of the Hemorrhissa incident. Keenan comments:

> When he touches the dead twelve-year-old daughter, the witnesses suddenly recognize that she has attained the age when menstruation begins. In both miracle stories, purity boundaries have been broken and so they become intimately linked by blood, touch, and number.

In four texts from the early centuries A.D. "the Hemorrhissa is identified as Berenice, a Macedonian version of the Greek name Pherenice, in Latin, Veronica" (p. 439). Finally, in the fourth-century *Acts of Pilate* it is said that the aforementioned Hemorrhissa/Berenice/Veronica spoke up at Jesus' trial to defend him on the basis of the miracle he had performed, but her testimony was disallowed because she was a woman.

Just as the bloody face of Jesus appears on Veronica's veil, so one woman's bleeding ceases, and another's begins. Jesus' face, whose appearance on Veronica's cloth is considered the true beginning of the artistic rendering of God in Christianity, must not be separated from these two women whose blood is linked to Jesus'. What this tells us is that the true story of the "true icon" is not that of a man as opposed to a woman, nor that of an image as opposed to a life, but about the synaesthetic unity of all of the above.

The original prints of both Veronicas in the *Miserere* suite are the only ones that are life-size. This conforms to our earlier statements regarding Rouault's insistence on the reality of this "true icon" and, as mentioned, its important relation to the Turin Shroud. As also mentioned, one should not separate the thick lines of the frame from the similarly thick "brush strokes" of the visage, for the cloth is not separate from the face but, rather, an essential part of the icon—indeed, it is the link between the original cloth and Rouault's "print." If Rouault's version has more power than others it is due, in part, to this integration of the cloth, which is no mere cloth. Truth be told, it is difficult—no, impossible—to determine the veil as such from the multiple planes and frames surrounding the face. One might even go so far as to say that there is no veil as such in either of the two images, although, of course there must be. Rouault's unwillingness to depict the veil as such, to separate it from the face itself, is, again, a testament to the enormous power of these two images, for the "true icon" transforms the mere cloth into the face rather than maintaining, as Fetti's and others' do, a separation between the two. We are drawn to the face as never before, as Rouault drew the face as never before. This is, indeed, a "true icon" and, as such, is synaesthetic in crossing over from a mere depiction to a reality that is not separate from us.

In the first of the two plates there is a radiance to the face from Rouault's use of light that is greatly diminished in the second whereas, in the second, there is a serenity that is greatly diminished in the first, if it is present there at all. Why, one must wonder, are these two Veronicas so different in this and other aspects, such as the fact that the two faces do not really even resemble each other? In the second image the lightest part of the print is relegated to one of the outer frames, whereas, in the first, the interior frame of light seems to emanate from Jesus' eyes, making the first image seem more "alive" than the second. Perhaps the two captions provide the answer. The first Veronica refers to Veronica's (and Jesus') "passing by" whereas the second (Isaiah 53:5) refers to our being healed by Jesus' wounds. The first, in other words, is meant to be a depiction of Jesus "en route" and so still living, whereas the second, which not coincidentally ends the entire series, is more "iconic" in representing the aftermath of Jesus' death, where the light has nearly gone out entirely but where we are "saved by his death, his wounds."

If verisimilitude becomes less important in modern art, that is because a higher, truer reality is achieved by emphasizing the expressivity of the work itself, not just what it represents outside itself. This higher reality is plainly evident in these two plates where the calligraphic power of the watercolor-like "brush strokes" give the holy face an almost tactile, three-dimensional force that is missing in more classical representations. The different planes of depth that are achieved by the artist's careful modulation of blacks, greys, and whites literally become the Medusa-like crown of barbed thorns that twist helplessly, and hopelessly, around the savior's head. Following in the footsteps of Manet and others in using the "brush strokes" and washes themselves to represent the crown, the hair, the beard, the brows, etc., Rouault succeeds in creating an image of Jesus that is as present as the ink itself. If, in the final words of the series that refer to the final plate, "we are healed by his wounds," we must synaesthetically feel those wounds for the "true image" to work. The Medusa-like terror and suffering must come alive in these images, as does, to be sure, the grace that this suffering engenders.

"*Lord, it is you . . .*" This grace is nowhere more evident than in the penultimate plate of the first half of the series, the one that precedes the first Veronica.

Figure 6.5 Georges Rouault, *Miserere*, pl. 32.

It is perhaps surprising that Rouault did not end the *Miserere* with this extraordinary plate rather than with the second Veronica. Not only would ending with one of the series' most refined prints make a certain artistic sense, but it would also make sense chronologically, for, as others have noted, this is the only image of the resurrected Christ in the entire *Miserere* series. And yet, as evident from other plates as well as the two Veronicas we have discussed, chronology is not a real concern for Rouault, and there is no arguing that ending each of the two parts with a Veronica makes sense as the aforementioned "image of an image," that is, as emblematic of all the other images.

This particular image of the resurrected Jesus is also, like the Veronicas, highly idiosyncratic in conforming to Rouault's own vision of this famous scene. First of all, we note how Rouault wisely eschews the customary, negative description of "Doubting Thomas" (the etymological link between "doubting" and "doubling" curiously doubles the name Thomas: "Thomas (Aramaic) and Didymus (Greek) both mean twin") by emphasizing the very moment when Thomas recognizes Jesus: "Seigneur, c'est vous, je vous reconnais" ("Lord, it is you, I recognize you!"). More important, though, is the fact that Rouault ignores the liturgical context of this moment by not only isolating Jesus and

Thomas but by placing them outside, "along the way," rather than indoors. This, I would argue, is not only because Rouault changes the story to suit his own inspired purpose, but because he again conflates the story with another related but different one.

The other, related event is the equally famous "Noli me tangere," "Do not touch me," as it is usually translated (more of this mistranslation later). In that scene, which appears in John in rapid succession with the later doubting Thomas scene, Jesus appeared first to Mary of Magdela, who had been left behind by the disciples to weep alone at Jesus' empty tomb:

> Now Mary stood outside the tomb crying. As she wept, she bent over to look into the tomb and saw two angels in white, seated where Jesus' body had been, one at the head and the other at the foot.
>
> They asked her, "Woman, why are you crying?"
>
> "They have taken my Lord away," she said, "and I don't know where they have put him." At this, she turned around and saw Jesus standing there, but she did not realize that it was Jesus.
>
> He asked her, "Why are you crying? Who is it you are looking for?"
>
> Thinking he was the gardener, she said, "Sir, if you have carried him away, tell me where you have put him, and I will get him."
>
> Jesus said to her, "Mary."
>
> She turned toward him and said, "Rabboni!" (which is Hebrew for "My Master").
>
> Jesus said, "Do not hold on to me, for I have not yet ascended to the Father. Go instead to my brothers and tell them, 'I am ascending to my Father and your Father, to my God and your God.'"
>
> Mary Magdalene went to the disciples with the news: "I have seen the Lord!" And she told them that he had said these things to her.

There are a number of ways in which it is clear that Rouault deliberately conflated these two, nearly adjacent stories (intervening is one paragraph describing Jesus' resurrected appearance to all the disciples except for Thomas). Textually there is Rouault's similar use of the term "Seigneur," "Lord" or "Master," which might not seem compelling if it were not the source of one of the greatest controversies in the history of Christianity. One of the main debates in the so-called Arian controversy was over whether Jesus was consubstantially the same as God, or whether, as Arius and his many persecuted followers insisted, he was not the same as God the Father but his only begotten son, a "Lord" and "Master" ("Kyrios") but not the same as God. Rouault's own textual inscription (while many of the captions in the series are direct quotes from scriptures and from other sources, this is not) seems to apply equally well to both scenes, in which the all-important moment of "recognition" is emphasized. And while the two stories seem to contradict one another insofar as Jesus wants Thomas to touch him but he wants Mary not to do so (*noli me tangere*), there is more similarity than difference here because, in both cases, there is reference to touching and, moreover, in the Thomas story Jesus clearly prefers not to be seen or touched when he admonishes Thomas for needing empirical proof: "Happy are they who never saw me and yet have found faith."

Pictorially speaking, Rouault's conflation of the two stories is even more evident. For in the famous painting by Correggio (a version of which Picasso had painted during his so-called "blue period"), as well as in other versions of this iconic scene, we discover a remarkable coincidence with Rouault's version.

Figure 6.6 *Noli me tangere* (1525), Correggio.

It is, I would argue, from these images that Rouault took his inspiration for the Thomas scene of *Miserere* pl. 32. Other similarities notwithstanding (e.g., in all these images Mary is reaching out to touch Jesus just as Thomas is doing; and in all there are only the two principals present), in all these images, and in particularly in the Correggio, Jesus' right arm and his upturned wrist are closely related in ways that have no relation to any of the famous depictions of the Thomas scene. And so, now that we know what we are looking at, what are the implications of Rouault's writing the story of Mary of Magdela into the story of "doubting Thomas?" And what are the implications of the conflation of these two stories regarding touching and not touching, and the importance (or not) of actually seeing Jesus, to our notion of art as synaesthetic and, here, of religion—or at least a certain form of religion—as synaesthetic in its concern with actually seeing, and touching, the divine?

Although it might seem that we have left behind the two Veronica images of the *Miserere*, and all that they entailed, this is surely not the case. First, we recall that the story of Veronica turned on touching Jesus, albeit (and this is important) through the buffer of a cloth, or veil. And we also recall that this story, according to certain commentators, is closely related—indeed, for some, identical—to the story of the Hemhorrissa, the woman whose bleeding stopped the moment that she surreptitiously touched Jesus' cloak. All these instances, then, involve touching of one sort or another, but they also all involve a certain negative, prohibitive view of touching Jesus. Even in the plate in question, which we have argued coalesces with the images of the *Noli me Tangere*, Rouault does not show Thomas touching Jesus. And finally, to add to this confusing array of scenes involving touching and not touching, there is the fact that, also in all these scenes, what is seen is not seen. That is to say, what is seen in all these cases is not what is really seen but, rather, what is un-seeable, a miracle: Jesus walking and talking after death, the "actual image" of Jesus appearing on the linen, the Hemorrhissa's bleeding ceasing after touching Jesus, the daughter of Jairus resurrected.

One way to make sense of all this is to recall that synaesthesia is also a non-touching touching, also seeing what is not really, or usually seen—also a miracle of sorts. In the plate in question, "Seigneur, c'est vous . . .," Jesus is not touched by Thomas because his "body" is transformed, has crossed over into the divine, into something that therefore cannot be touched even if/when it is touched.[10] The numerous prohibitions against touching or seeing the divine can be understood in synaesthetic terms as prohibitions against seeing or touching an "All" that is incapable of being seen or touched as such. Religion and art, however, can resolve this by showing what cannot be shown (the actual face of Jesus), by touching without actually touching because actual touching is never really actual touching insofar as touching is inherently synaesthetic in bringing together two things as one.

In "Seigneur, c'est vous . . ." there is a decided contrast between the face of the lowly disciple and Jesus' look of total beatitude. Moreover, Jesus seems to float above Thomas, existing in a very different space than that of his doubtful disciple. But, perhaps, we should invoke the curious doublings referred to earlier, of a Thomas/Didyma who is double and of a doubting that is etymologically "double." In this respect, this image is not so much of two different people but, rather, of all human beings insofar as they are doubled by a "higher," miraculous, synaesthetic self and an ordinary, mundane identity that is filled with doubt that such things as the miracle of synaesthesia, the miracle of the "true icon," the miracle of true art that is inherently synaesthetic in providing a vision of something that cannot be seen with our ordinary eyes.

7

Feeling/Hearing Picasso: The Synaesthetics of Cubism and the Vollard Suite

"He wants us to drink gasoline, spit fire and eat tow."

Braque on Picasso

At the same time (1933) that Picasso was at work on etchings for the now-famous "Vollard suite," the photographer Brassaï visited the painter's sculpture studio:

> Cubism was born under the banner of exacerbated plasticity. It is the work of a man who has become polarized, in the most natural manner, towards *fullness of form. Cubism gave the sensation of a sculpture that rotated, simultaneously revealing its different facets.* (italics mine)[1]

While many have attributed the shift in style away from Picasso's earlier, cubist works to the artist's Protean genius, we will attempt to bring together Picasso's more "classical" later works with the same synaesthetic sensibility that characterizes cubism. In the first part of this chapter we will discuss cubism itself ("Feeling Picasso") as synaesthetic, and then, in the second part ("Hearing Picasso") we will attempt a synaesthetic reading of Picasso's most famous suite of etchings—indeed, according to many, the most famous series of etchings in modern art.

Feeling Picasso: The Mandolin Player. A photograph of Picasso's studio on the Boulevard Raspail taken in 1913 shows a large cubist collage Picasso was working on from which a number of actual items—a small guitar, a newspaper, and so on—are hanging.

Figure 7.1 Collage by Picasso in his studio on the Boulevard Raspail, 1913.

What is telling about this photograph is not that Picasso included actual objects *in* his paintings; there is certainly nothing new in that. What is telling is that Picasso included actual objects *on* his paintings. That is to say, in the extraordinary collages and "analytic" cubist works of the first decades of the twentieth century, objects outside the painting are no longer merely represented in the painting. Rather, the point of so-called "cubism" is to present—not represent—the actual object in the painting (hence the related importance of collages and "ready-mades") in order to feel the object's presence rather than just to see it. There are many conflicting theories about cubism, and many debates about the relative validity of these theories, but the "theory" that we will examine here is that there is no "theory" of cubism (*theorein* = "to see") because the whole goal of cubism is to replace the seen object with a synaesthetic experience that is more felt than seen.

We must, then, dismiss many of the prevalent theories of cubism—beginning with a superficial name that was coined merely as a matter of convenience. Nor is cubism to be understood abstractly or, in the words of John Berger, as a sort of "mechanical diagram," "the diagram being a visible symbolic representation of invisible processes, forces, structures." There is nothing "abstract" about the equally inaptly named "abstract art," and that is particularly the case with "cubism." *Rather, cubism is an attempt to experience the object with more than just the eyes.* Like "abstract" art in general, it feels the color or object more concretely, not less, and to avoid the trap of turning that very concreteness into an abstraction, it is necessary to approach both cubism and abstract art in general as synaesthetic in replacing what is merely seen with what is experienced tactually.

Figure 7.2 Girl with Mandolin, 1910.

Notwithstanding the obvious synesthetic coupling of this and many other "cubist" paintings that incorporate musical themes,[2] what we are looking at in this "painting" of Picasso is not the figure as such—that *would* be abstract—but, rather, all the shapes, line, forms, and, above all, tones that function like synaesthesia in replacing the one known object with a kaleidoscope of other "objects" that don't so much shatter the mandolin player as such as render her more complete. In this painting one can understand the well-known resistance of Picasso and Braque to the pure "abstraction" of other cubists working around this time, because for the former the "object" is important precisely because it isn't important, whereas, for those like Delauney, the absence of any recognizable object might not be as powerful because it does not "deconstruct" the object as such. That being said, perhaps too much should not be made of this distinction, because the freedom to express a reality that is its own, and that expresses what I am referring to as a synaesthetic versus a merely aesthetic reality, is evident in both cases.

In this painting it is the "fullness of form" that matters, and this fullness cannot, by definition, be found in what is merely seen. The oft-noted relation of cubism to sculpture, and particularly Picasso's own sculptures, cubist and otherwise, is very important in this regard, for both media are used to try and touch the viewer with this fullness of form rather than distancing the viewer by allowing him/her to merely see the "object."

Figure 7.3 Head of a woman, 1909–10.

In *Girl with Mandolin* one could comment, easily enough, on the many interesting formal, compositional devices such as, for example, the way the woman's two breasts, one full, the other flipped open as if in the midst of a mastectomy (Picasso!), parallels the two parts of the mandolin, the one full, the other (the neck of the instrument) attenuated. But the more important point that Picasso is making with this device is to make us *feel* the depth of the object more concretely, not to think it. In analyzing this work one could also easily, if heretically, ignore the usual generic classifications and see in it a link to the "expressionism" of van Gogh and others that we know heavily influenced Picasso even before the "Cézanne-effect" hit him. The heavily contrasted zones of light and dark that both inform and deform the "object" are almost De Kooning-like in forcing us to feel what we are seeing. To paraphrase Magritte: "This is not a mandolin player," not because it isn't (any more than Magritte's painting "is not a pipe"), but because, like any great painting, the object seen is not merely the object seen. Rather, in this painting it is the sculptural sensations felt by the textured jumble of forms that turn painting into the synaesthetic fullness of sculpture.

In *Girl with Mandolin* Picasso wisely refrained from introducing any color that would interfere with this tactile, sculptural effect. In an example of the later, more colorful use of "cubist" techniques one can see how successfully Picasso was able to integrate color into his ability to render this same synaesthetic fullness of form.

Figure 7.4 Three Musicians, 1921.

As in *Girl with Mandolin*, the "object" or objects have been replaced by textured layers that are here enhanced by the use of color. The lighter tones of the clarinet player are perhaps purposefully rendered in white, but that is not to argue for a cheap musical allegorization of the synaesthetic effect we are arguing for here. Rather, the "music" of the painting is to be found in the different tones of the painting—the whites, the harlequinesque red and yellow, the incomprehensible "blues," etc. The ominous, Arbus-like masks staring out at us remove any trace of lightheartedness here; instead, the relatively inhuman tones and shapes create their own "music" in the careful modulation of the different color zones: the white on the left, the red and yellow pattern in the middle, the black on the right, all join with the other colors in feeling the music that we cannot see or hear. The synaesthetic experience is particularly evident in the musical score, which is less a musical reference than a reference to the lines and grids that have replaced the faces of two of the musicians—shapes, in other words, that are sounds, and sounds that are shapes.

Hearing Picasso: The Vollard Suite. Picasso's most famous suite of etchings amply demonstrates Derrida's argument about "drawings of the blind" discussed in an earlier chapter. The particular power of these etchings is not just the oft-mentioned extraordinary draughtsmanship and other technical aspects of these works—like the suite of "etchings" discussed in the previous chapter that Rouault completed for Vollard a few years before Picasso began his series, these graphic works greatly expanded the usual boundaries of etchings and lithography. Nor is it just that of the many biographical references that the suite's few commentators have been largely content to explore: Picasso's sexuality, his relation to Marie-Thérèse, etc. Rather, it is the synaesthetic language that one hears spoken by the 100 etchings themselves, 100 etchings which, like Dante's 100 cantos or Boccaccio's 100 stories, tell us a great deal more than merely "meets the eye." It is readily apparent to the viewer that in this extraordinary suite of drawings Picasso is no longer merely drawing (if that were ever really the case), but also saying something to those "with ears to hear."

We will limit our interpretation here to two etchings, one from each of the two largest of the four sections of the work. These four sections are: "the artist and his model" (the largest, made up of some forty-six pieces), "the tauromachia," "the minotaur," and to round out the 100, two portraits of the art dealer Vollard, which appear like the two cover pages of a book where one finds the customary publication information.

As mentioned before, it would be easy enough to argue for the synaesthetic quality of the sculptural works of the 1930s that Picasso was at work on while also drawing these etchings. In particular, the bulbous distended face, with that famous cranial nose, of Marie-Thérèse that dominates both media reminds us of the "fullness of form" Brassaï was referencing, but which we can explain further as the tactile rendering of what the figure feels like in addition to what the "object" looks like.

Figure 7.5 Bust Marie-Thérèse, 1931.

It is, indeed, no coincidence that this and similar sculptures were made at the same time as the etchings. The image just shown was part of a two-page spread from Minotaure #1 that positioned the sculpture opposite three of *the Vollard Suite* etchings, as if looking at them in the way that, throughout the suite, the "sculptor" is seen staring at his sculptures. Adding to the *trompe l'oeil* effect found throughout the suite of images looking at images, the very same sculpture is repeated in the etching (*the Vollard Suite* # 38).

Figure 7.6 Pl. 38 Sculptor Reclining #1.

The *trompe l'oeil* of this and many of the 100 etchings is itself a kind of synaesthesia, for as we gaze at the image of *the Vollard Suite* 38 we realize that we are looking at the etched figures the same that they (or in this case, the "sculptor") are looking at the sculpted figure. The sculptor is and is not Picasso, for although there is no physical resemblance between the Jove-like figure and Picasso, we know that he is the sculptor of the figure of Marie-Thérèse. Similarly, we are and are not Picasso, because we are placed in his position by looking at the etching the same way that "Picasso" is looking at his sculpture. The etching thus immediately places us in a vortex of identities that belies its simplicity just as it belies our position inside and outside the work, and inside and outside the artist. (It was Longinus, the "classical" literary philosopher, who made the statement that the spectator who truly appreciates a work of art—we might call him/her the "connoisseur"—becomes the artist who created the work in question.)

It is telling that Picasso did not recreate the bust in its original size, but actually made it as the same size, or perhaps even smaller, than the sculptor and his model. The reason for this, I believe, is that the tactile sensation of the larger bust is taken over by the "real" figures; the sculptor's conspicuous left hand, for example, is larger by itself than Marie-Thérèse's entire bust. Indeed, the two nude bodies can be felt in their embrace, for both figures are "full" and thereby give the viewer a very strong sensation of their felt presence. In other words, the two etched figures take over the fullness of the sculpted figure in providing the viewer with a felt sensation that is even stronger than the "actual" physical presence of the sculpted figure. And yet, in placing all three figures together Picasso is thereby emphasizing the unity as well as the difference between sculpture and etching and, one might add, between the two "classical" figures and their decidedly more abstract, modern creation, as if to say that the different media, like the different periods, are as unified synaesthetically as the different sensations in question.

So much for the physical presence and presences, the formidable "fullness of form," in the etching. One must also *hear* the significant expressions on the faces of the etched figures, as opposed to the sculpted figure who, like her actual sculpted counterparts, bears no such expression. Throughout the Suite we find countless examples of such expressivity, something that Picasso the painter learned from his classical predecessors. Although many point to the influence of Greek vase painting and other ancient sources on these etchings, those figures are also decidedly lacking in the facial expressivity that emerges in the Renaissance but which is even more readily seen in painters such as Ingres. In the closing pages of his perceptive essay "The Parabola of the Sculptor," Francisco Seraller argues for the importance of the "pseudoclassical" Ingres to Picasso's "Sculptor's Studio" etchings that make up such a large part of *the Vollard Suite*, and the numerous illustrations he offers to support his thesis reveal a similar sensibility in both artists that goes far beyond their stunningly graceful, expert draughtsmanship. Looking at *Raphael and Fornarina*, for example, one immediately feels the same delicate, "classical" drama of the two personages that one repeatedly finds in *the Vollard Suite*. Raphael is looking at his painting of Fornarina while holding the "real" figure on his lap; she, on the other hand, is gazing at the viewer with both the look of a model and the proud, tender look of the great artist's mistress.

Figure 7.7 Raphael and La Fornarina, 1814.

The resemblance to the Picasso etchings is, indeed, striking. In the etching just shown, the sculptor, also embracing his model, is staring at his sculpture while she stares directly at the viewer. There are, of course, important differences: the Vollard Suite etchings are linked to sculpture by virtue of the "sculptural" qualities of both, whereas Ingres links painting to painting (another indication of the importance of sculpture-as-etching to Picasso during this period). Moreover, the love that seems so readily apparent in *Raphael and Fornarina* is replaced, in *the Vollard Suite* 38, with a coarser sensuality that one would expect from Picasso. Nonetheless, what unites both works, and the *Vollard Suite* in general with many of Ingres' paintings (above all, the famous *Bather of Valpancon*), is the poignant but muted drama that Picasso, too, injects into all these works. Even the somewhat disengaged gaze of the sculptor (compared to the more focused look of his model) is telling in this regard: his more stoic gaze reminds us of one of Picasso's most famous adages that "one should take pleasure everywhere, except in one's own work."

In discussing this Picasso/Ingres connection, Seraller quotes approvingly Michel Leiris' statement that Picasso didn't just paint people and objects but "embraced them with the eyes": "Exactly! Embrace with the eyes! This is the essential act and parabola . . . of all artistic creation—see the story of Pygmalion" (46). If Picasso's "Sculptor's Studio" etchings are a sort of reversal of the Pygmalion myth in which real people and things turn into artworks, the difference is not that great after all. For, either way, the artwork reverses the familiar Platonic denigration by making art more real than mere reality by synaesthetically "embracing" what is not to be touched—even in the case of sculpture. "Embrace with the eyes" refers to the fact that, in Picasso as in Ingres, one doesn't merely see these works; rather, one can feel them, and one can hear their muted whisperings, if only one listens carefully enough.

Figure 7.8 Pl 59 Bacchic Scene with Minotaur.

Although the "Sculptor's Studio" constitutes the largest part—forty-six—of the *Vollard Suite*'s hundred etchings, the other major section of the Suite dealing with images of the Minotaur is equally synaesthetic in compelling us to hear and feel its curious message. In these strange images, stranger still when the different views of the man-beast are taken together, one is reminded of the importance of their classical, and even pre-classical sources. Unlike the fifty-eight prints of Georges Rouault's *Miserere* series discussed earlier (also commissioned by Vollard), these etchings must be approached with a different god—or rather gods—in mind. For these works are true to a pre-Christian sensibility that has little or nothing to do with the Christian tradition (indeed, Picasso's entire oeuvre is largely anti-religious when compared to contemporaries, including Matisse). Rather, the minotaur is viewed far less morally or judgmentally, and with far more reverence and awe than that of the mere monster he was to become. More bluntly: when we look at some of these decidedly "incorrect" images, where the minotaur routinely fondles, rapes, and is himself adored by his female objects of desire, we must remember that the sensibility here is as pagan as the Málagan himself.

But the minotaur was also embraced by moderns other than Picasso. We have already mentioned that one of the first discussions of these etchings, and the sculptures Picasso was working on at the same time, appeared in the first issue of the important surrealist *Minotaure*. With the connection to surrealism, and especially Breton (who contributed an essay on Picasso to that same issue), we are reminded of the Freudian connection to this more favorable reappraisal of the so-called monster. Just as Freud argued for the persistence of a "Minoan" substratum of thought that predates not only Christianity but any moral consciousness whatsoever (including Platonism), so too the surrealists in general, and Picasso in particular, identified artistic creativity with an un-conscious that eschews, not only moral judgments, and not only consciousness in general but, most importantly for our purposes, the separation of consciousness from a synaesthetic unconscious that reunites humanity with the greater unity of all its thoughts and sensations. In this sense, the minotaur represents a greater fullness than that of our so-called normal humanity.

Let us keep this sensibility in mind when approaching the particular etching that we have chosen for discussion here. As is the case with many of Picasso's minotaur etchings, the head of the beast is dark (cf., in particular, #58, the more tender "Minotaur Caressing a Sleeping Woman"), not because Picasso had to depict the bull this way, but to represent the bull's greater physical, material presence. This is confirmed by the other "dark center" of the etching, where the Bacchic reveler's bearded face is similarly darkened. This similarity is also indicative of the Freudian interpretation of the minotaur just mentioned, namely, the minotaur as a projection of an un- or pre-conscious, "dark" part of humanity. And, while the two writhing women are as "white" as their male counterparts are not, Picasso does make a significant exception in darkening the women's pubic areas—more so in the case of the minotaur's "partner," whose vagina is centered between his lips and the glass that the Bacchic reveler is holding up for a toast.

The affinity—indeed, if I am correct, identity—between the minotaur and the Bacchic reveler is also evident in their similar postures: not only are they both holding wine glasses, but in each case the wine glass is held similarly (the "two-fingered" style) and the arms are similarly poised atop their legs, as if to emphasize the pure physicality—body upon body upon body—of the scene as well as the mirroring of the two "men" in which the minotaur raises his glass with his left hand, the reveler with his right. Indeed, the circular writhing of the swooning women, with their own voluptuous curves accentuated by their curving motions, gives added emphasis to the fullness of the scene's physical presence.

And yet, in showing them as holding their glasses out, and holding themselves up more vertically than their female counterparts, Picasso is also departing somewhat from the pure physicality of the scene. However, a civilized gesture such as the toast, and, indeed, the mere difference between a "vertical" civilization from a "horizontal" earthiness, should not be seen in oppositional terms. Here heaven and hell, sex and religion, are conjoined—just as they are conjoined in myths about Olympian gods such as Zeus and Apollo routinely indulging their most libidinal desires.

Although he does not always do so, in this particular etching Picasso depicts the minotaur as a much larger figure than that of the reveler. Perhaps this is less indicative of the minotaur's great size than of the Bacchic reveler's smaller stature, for satyr figures which are the model and particular "type" of this reveler are usually small. But, whatever the reason, the phallic "thrusts" of the minotaur's two arms (especially the right one, which is "holding up," as it were, the entire scene) and the minotaur's more imposing presence make his dominance over the entire scene undeniable.

What, one wonders, is being toasted? Who, one wonders, was the first to raise his glass? Given that the minotaur's glass is higher, and that his arm is more outstretched, one would have to say the minotaur has initiated the gesture. This brings us into the real heart, the real drama of the scene, which is not that of the orgiastic "foursome" but, as in the case of the other etching and the relevant Ingres painting just discussed, the particular *looks* of the four principals. The minotaur's "mistress" is looking at the viewers with what appears to be a faint smile. In keeping with her dance-like posture (typical in Picasso's oeuvre), the reveler's eyes are cast directly upward, also away from the scene itself. The eyes of the reveler and minotaur, somewhat surprisingly, are also similarly detached; neither of them—indeed, none of the four—is looking at each other nor, for that matter, at any of the four principals. For this is not a human scene at all. We are reminded of the discomfort animals feel if their eyes are engaged in a "stare," because such staring is associated with danger, with the threat of predation. Here the looks are all disengaged because, unlike the *trompe l'oeil* effect discussed earlier, we are looking at a scene where what is being communicated has nothing whatsoever to do with mere looking. Even our own position, as lookers, is belied by a scene which is less about what one sees than what one "embraces with the eyes."

Finally, one must contrast the two distracted looks of the minotaur and the reveler and note, in particular, the greater poignancy of the minotaur's blank gaze. The reveler is smiling as he gazes off into space—doubtless the result of inebriation, not of any "deep thinking." The minotaur, however, is not smiling in return. Indeed, if one looks closely at his eye (we only see one), we see what appears to be a tear, the same tear that symbolizes the melancholy of all these etchings in general and, in particular, that of the impending doom that is inevitably to befall the minotaur, whether from Theseus or, in these etchings, in the arena. For the minotaur's greater physical, sexual, violent presence is doomed by a humanity to whose unconscious he and his synaesthetic fullness of being are destined to be relegated.

8

Georgia O'Keeffe and the Music of Flowers

Figure 8.1 *Music: Pink and Blue No. 2.*

In an oeuvre where the boundaries between flowers and non-flowers, between representation and abstraction, are largely irrelevant, does it matter that *Music: Pink and Blue No. 2* is not one of O'Keeffe's famous "flower paintings?" No, for, as the Whitney Catalogue accompanying a recent (2004) exhibition of her "abstract" works notes, "Abstraction allowed her to express intangible experience—be it a quality of light, color, sound, or response to a person or place."[1] Like Paul Klee, ordinary reality and the ordinary objects are less real than these so-called "abstractions." As O'Keeffe herself stated: "Nothing is less real than so-called realism."

We will treat the painting above as representative of the large number of "flower paintings" in the artist's oeuvre. Our indifference to this "difference without a difference" is also warranted by our reading of art, and particularly O'Keeffe's art, as synaesthetic, as inherently indifferent to the usual boundaries separating things and senses from one another. Less daring, to be sure, is our choice of this painting as an example of "art as synaesthesia," for this work of 1918–1919 is entitled *Music: Pink and Blue No. 2.*[2]

The relationship between music and painting is both subtle and obvious, particularly in the case of O'Keeffe. With respect to her own work in general, we know that she embraced the practice of her teacher at the Teacher's College at Columbia University who asked his students to paint the music they were listening to,[3] stating later that this gave her "the idea that I was very interested to follow later—the idea that music could be translated into something for the eye."[4] And the relationship between music and painting in O'Keeffe's work also goes the other way, with critics like William Murrell Fisher commenting on the music they hear in O'Keeffe's "silent" paintings:

> Of all things earthly, it is only in music that one finds any analogy to the emotional content of these drawings—to the gigantic, swirling rhythms, and the exquisite tenderness so powerfully and sensitively rendered—and music is the condition toward which . . . all art constantly aspires.[5]

The notion of "visual music" was very much in the air among the avant-garde artists that had gathered around Alfred Stieglitz in New York in the early decades of the twentieth century. Marsden Hartley, for example, a painter of the "Stieglitz circle" whom O'Keeffe admired, wrote that "Kandinsky [in *On the Spiritual in Art*] is attempting to paint the color of sound," and "with a sense also of the color of sound as I get those feelings out of music . . . I have even done something after a prelude of César Franck's."[6] Kandinsky is exemplary for this treatise on art as synaesthesia in creating works that are both explicitly titled with musical names, like the present work of O'Keeffe's we are discussing, and works that, while not titled musically, nonetheless demonstrate the "quasi-synaesthetic" essence of all art. (Despite rumors to the contrary, Kandinsky was not a synesthete.) Indeed, we might add to our oft-repeated thesis concerning the similarity between art and synaesthesia the corollary that if art that is explicitly synaesthetic is not often great art, this is because a strong neurological crossover destroys the necessary distance that is required to experience the artwork as such.

Another member of the Steitglitz circle who must be mentioned in the context of "visual music" is Arthur Dove, the painter whom O'Keeffe famously referred to as the one other member of the circle whose works she could look at for months, as opposed to merely days or weeks in the case of Hartley and John Marin. The reason for O'Keeffe's approval is not hard to fathom, for Dove's "abstract representationality" most closely resembles O'Keeffe's own abstract/concrete pictorial visions. Moreover, the two shared a similar attitude toward "visual music" that expressed itself both theoretically ("Anybody should be able to feel a certain state and express it in terms of paint or music . . . [Art] is nearer to music." Dove[7]) as well as in the titles of their paintings; in Dove's case, titles like "Sentimental Music" (1913), "Chinese Music" (1923), and "Primitive Music" (1944).

One of Dove's paintings that O'Keeffe might have pondered at some length is *Fog Horns* (1929), a painting that Judith Zilcher[8] singled out as "one of the most convincing synaesthetic paintings in the history of early modernism".

Figure 8.2

What draws Ms. Zilcher's interest in this particular painting is no doubt the close affinity between the titular sound of "foghorns" and the three circles that seem to correspond perfectly to the sounds of three foghorn blasts on the ocean. In Dove's other paintings, and, indeed, in most of the examples of abstract works with musical titles (including O'Keeffe's), the connection between the images and their musical referents is tenuous at best, for example, Mondrian's famous *Broadway Boogie Woogie*. But Dove's painting, like all the others of this kind, is not really an image of the sound in question; even Zilcher herself only goes so far as to claim that such works "conjure," "suggest," "evoke," etc. their musical referents. Rather than arguing for any synaesthetic identification between sight and sound, then, we are dealing with "affinities" that, as argued in the Introduction to this work, are only really identifications insofar as they are catachreses—that is, possibilities that are actualities in an aesthetic realm that is defined not by actualities but possibilities that are made actualities. In this respect, the foghorns can, indeed, be heard in Dove's painting, even though they represent the quasi-synaesthesia of all art. (This gives new meaning to Aristotle's insistence that true art presents possible impossibilities, versus impossible possibilities.[9])

Music does not really exist insofar as it only "exists" in motion, and such motion defies the static nature of thought in defining existence or any existent as such. If there is music in *Music—Pink and Blue II,* it is less apparent in the painting itself than when it is viewed alongside the paintings O'Keeffe produced immediately before this one: *Music: Pink and Blue #1,* as well as *Over Blue,* the pastel on paper that one assumes to be a preliminary version of the two oils that immediately followed.

Figure 8.3

Figure 8.4

Viewed together, the modulation of these three similar works (which unfortunately appear less similar due to the faulty reproductions of the colors) does, indeed, produce a kind of musical movement in the works' subtle variations of line and color. Was that, one wonders, the source of O'Keeffe's musical titles, as opposed to any musical referent in the individual works? We know that Dove, for example, and others did create individual works that were meant to be viewed diachronically rather than synchronically in order to create the effect of listening to music over time. But if there is music in the individual paintings it is, rather, to be found in their "abstract" freedom from any referent and their expression, instead, of pure colors, textures, and tones—terms that all, not coincidentally, apply to music as well as to paintings such as these.

Although the "music" of these works, taken individually, "exists" in their color, texture, line, and tone insofar as, like music, those are freed from their identification with any objects as such, this freedom also allows for the identification of certain important aspects of nature, particularly those of the sky in all three and (as we argued), the flower in *Music—Pink and Blue II*. It is the presence of these natural elements that makes O'Keeffe's works so successful, and why she preferred Dove's similarly "hybrid" concrete/abstractions to those of others, such as Hartley. It is as if the painter were aware of the fact that to be free to "abstract" pure color, line, and tone also means to be free to include those elements of nature, for, otherwise, one is not really free. The synaesthesia of these paintings, then, lies in their connection to things such as the sky and the flower while, at the same time, their avoidance of the same. In this respect one could say that *Music—Pink and Blue II* is as much, if not more, of a flower than any of O'Keeffe's flower paintings per se. (We will return to the subject of what these paintings do and do not represent, including the well-known controversy of the sexuality of O'Keeffe's flower paintings, in the next section of this chapter.)

If one were to try and describe *Music—Pink and Blue II* it would be essential to avoid merely talking about what one sees, for to do so would doom any discussion of the experience of this painting from the outset. One could only describe the experience thus: it is "to hear the sound of the sky through the music of the flower." For, as evident from an examination of O'Keeffe's numerous other works that depict the azure of the sky less ambiguously (particularly after her visits, and later move, to New Mexico starting in the late 1920s), we are experiencing the sky-not-sky through the flower-not-flower. It is, I would argue, just as difficult not to see this painting (and the other two just mentioned) as floral as it is not to see the blue, with its flecks and wisps of cloudlike white, as "sky-al." The thick, pedal-like borders of the "flower's" various folds are indisputably those of a flower. But, to paraphrase Magritte's famous notion, "This is (not) a flower." And it is precisely in its not being a flower, and in the sky not being the sky, that allows the music of the painting to be heard. For since the objects we are seeing are not really the objects we are seeing, we must, instead, feel the textures, lines, and colors in their soft and supple embrace of the sky that, as in the Greek temple,[10] comes to life not in its separation from, but in its unity with, the beauty it bestows upon the flower. Having once again invoked Heidegger, we might also say that what we are experiencing in this work is the very sound of Being, as opposed to the ordinary sounds of beings: "Like hearing the voice of a friend, that every being carries along with it" ("*als hören die Stimme des Freundes, das jedes Dasein bei sich trägt*")[11].

* * *

Figure 8.5

Everyone is familiar with the controversy of O'Keeffe's flowers.[12] The comparison of these works—which are, after all, of sexual organs of a kind—to female genitalia is long-standing, as well as part of a general view of her work as overtly female. Already, in the 1920s, O'Keeffe's "gloriously female" paintings were seen as "anchored in the constitution of the woman. *The organs that differentiate the sex speak.*"[13] Both those who argue for the sexual content of these works (e.g., "It now seems abundantly clear that, in spite of her vehement denials, O'Keeffe meant some of her paintings (not just the flowers) to look vaginal"[14]) and those, like O'Keeffe herself, who reject such an identification, are correct, and it is by approaching this problem in terms of synaesthesia and, particularly, of O'Keeffe's paintings as a kind of visual music that we will be able to resolve this apparent contradiction.

We can certainly forgive O'Keeffe for being unable to answer questions about the symbolism of her flower paintings. She was caught in an intellectual double bind that would be difficult for anyone, let alone an extremely bright but, ultimately, very practical artist who was not given to the sort of theorizing that one finds in an artist like Kandinsky. If she had said "yes, the paintings are vaginal," or even if she left the matter ambiguous, she would have encountered both moral outrage (keeping in mind that many of these paintings were done before women had finally achieved the right to vote) and, what would have been worse for her, an unbearable one-sidedness in approaches to her entire oeuvre as well as to the individual paintings themselves. On the other hand, if she said "no way!" as she adamantly did, she would merely be denying one of the many "truths in painting" that everyone—including O'Keeffe—knew was there. Since the first option left O'Keeffe with no way out, she chose the latter, for at least that left her and the integrity of her artworks relatively intact. In other words: since there is no more way to be a "little vaginal" than there is to be a "little pregnant," O'Keeffe was forced to deny the truth altogether. But, as friend and contemporary D. H. Lawrence is well known to have said: "Never trust the teller, trust the tale."

As representative of these works I have again chosen a painting (above) that is not that of a flower per se, but, as one writer notes: "It is looked upon as one of her best works. Is it a floral painting? Is it a close up of the inner part of a flower? It is this ambiguity which is fascinating and has led some critics to argue that it is an abstract work and that the undulating folds are based upon female genitalia."[15] Another painting from this period (before O'Keeffe turned away from her obsessive painting of flowers) clearly demonstrates the irrelevance of this distinction.

Figure 8.6

The key, I believe, to resolving this long-standing controversy is to recognize that, while many of these works, and particularly many of the flowers, are vaginal (or, more properly, vulval), they are also so much more. No one is going to prevent even the youngest children from viewing these paintings, and no one is going to place them in an obscure corner of the Orsay or behind curtains in the manner of Courbet's famous depiction of "The Origin of the World." Nor is it the case that the vaginal significance is some kind of "secret meaning," for it is at once "manifest and latent," to use the Freudian terminology that is often in play when critics, and O'Keeffe herself, discussed the paintings' sexuality. In one of Freud's statements that is never mentioned with regard to this controversy, the founder of psychoanalysis (and someone whose works were well known by Stieglitz and his circle, including O'Keeffe[16]) remarked on the odd fact that "the sight of the genitals is rarely considered beautiful."[17] The reason for this, in psychoanalytical terms, is that repression denies the beauty of our most essential source of sexuality. Therefore, since no one on either side of the controversy would deny the beauty of these works, one would have to conclude that O'Keeffe has accomplished something marvelous, indeed, in not only creating artistic masterpieces but also in overcoming one of civilization's greatest taboos in rendering female genitalia—the "pudenda," "that of which one should be ashamed,"—not only as "that of which one should NOT be ashamed," but as "that which is beautiful."

These "vaginal" artworks are not just marginally significant in O'Keeffe's oeuvre; they are, in fact, among her finest works. They are among her most essential paintings because they represent something essential in her unique, individual genius, namely, the synaesthetic secretions of a profound physicality that stems from an erotic "pleasure principle" that informs all art. (This is why Freud saw in art a unique window into the unconscious as well as amassing a huge collection of artworks himself.) There is no choosing, then, between the vaginal and the non-vaginal interpretations of these paintings. It is essential that they be both because, like music, they represent the pleasure of the body in concert with the mind before the invidious "mind/body dichotomy" severed our fundamental, synaesthetic unity—a severing that is plainly evident in renderings, such as Caravaggio's, of the Medusa, herself a symbol of the horror of female genitalia in a male-dominated age of reason.

9

Joan Mitchell and the Power of Blue

In her recent biographical study of Joan Mitchell—the first such work of its kind[1]—Patricia Albers argued that "Mitchell had both synaesthesia and an eidetic memory. In other words, Mitchell saw much of the world—letters, sounds, people, and even emotions—as colors, while at the same time remembering every detail of the past as vividly as the present."[2] Although Albers does not conclusively prove her hypothesis, this does not undermine the thesis that we have put forth in the present work that actual synaesthesia—whether Joan Mitchell's or that of van Gogh,[3] who was one of Mitchell's constant and profound inspirations—is less of an issue in art than the idea that art, rather than the artist, is synaesthetic.

The color synaesthesia in Mitchell's work that Albers argues for is the most common among the eighty or so different kinds of actual, neurological synaesthesia and, moreover, of all those forms of color synaesthesia, blue is the color referred to most in studies of the clinical condition. (Note the prevalence of such references in titles like *Wednesday is Indigo Blue*, *The Frog who Croaked Blue*, *Blue Cats and Chartreuse Kittens*, etc.) Reflecting this tendency, the fact that blue is also the color most closely associated with Joan Mitchell could be used to support Albers' "revelation," although that is not to say that it dominates every Mitchell painting any more than it dominates every form of color synaesthesia.

We have previously (Chapter 5) discussed the many paintings of Klee that return writing to its original status as a concrete thing in which "word and image come together at the origin of both."[4] Klee's "secret alphabet" magically creates a writing that is not writing as such but letters, words, diacritical marks, etc., before they have been reduced to mere "signifiers" or "signifieds." They are, as Freud posited, like the concrete word-things that appear in dreams. Although Joan Mitchell's paintings might, at first view, appear further from such *écritures/peintures* than Klee's or, for that matter, from those of Joan Mitchell's close friend and associate Franz Kline, they too are a "secret alphabet" in which every mark is replete with a sort of calligraphic meaning that belies the separation between signifier and signified, form and content, that is anathema to all art. As Véronique Fóti argues in her insightful discussion of "Adversity and Practices of Painting: Merleau-Ponty, Monet, and Joan Mitchell," "abstract" expressionists like Joan Mitchell "undercut the classical distinction between *disegno*, prized in Renaissance Florence, and color, prized by the Venetian school,"[5] but the erasure of this "classical distinction" applies not only to Joan Mitchell but, as Heidegger and others have argued,[6] to all art insofar as it belies the separation between form and content or, in this case, line and color.

Failure to see this, failure to see the paintings as synaesthetic language in which line and color, color and meaning, merge ("Blue is Joan Mitchell") is as mistaken as taking the paintings as ordinary script that would convey the ordinary meanings that are all too often used to describe "Mitchell's poignant visual searching" (55):

> Black paint heightens a paradoxical sense of sadness and liberation. This sublime landscape may express Mitchell's momentary discovery of the serenity of death.[7]
>
> The paintings are a revelation of irresoluble tensions in experience and feeling and are, in Françoise-Claire Proudhon's estimation, comparable to Proustian imagery in giving sensory form to emotional experience.[8]

Mitchell paints word-and-images that convey meaning through their material "signifiers" before it has been wrested from their grasp. What, then, is the "meaning" of these paintings? Why is this meaning synaesthetic, as opposed to merely aesthetic? And, why the predominance of the color blue?

Beauvais (1986)

Figure 9.1

The first thing that might strike the "naïve" viewer of *Beauvais*[9] is its book-like appearance. Studies of Joan Mitchell's work often note the importance of poetry and poets in her life; she was close friends with Frank O'Hara, John Ashberry, and Samuel Beckett, and, as stated above, "Joan . . . was well aware that her works were 'poetry in the form of painting' or 'music in the form of painting.'" While the enormous size of the two panels, as well as their discontinuous relation, makes us wonder why they are presented together rather than apart, I would add to the view taken by some, that such multiple panels represent movement, the idea that we are looking at an illustrated book, one where the illustration *is* the book rather than separate from it, and where the relation of the two paintings is one in which the same letters and words of one page are used to say something else on the next page.

The influence of Cézanne, especially that of the late water colors "in which the total immersion in nature, the unfinished element, the breaking up, the disgregation [*sic*] and the disintegration of the world . . . would become fundamental in Joan Mitchell's work,"[10] is evident here, but so is the departure from one of her acknowledged masters. "By taking a decisive step away from the painted form to the autonomous brushstroke or gesture, she appeared to be expressing a radically changed view of what painting is. Color and composition no longer served Mitchell as a means of creating illusions in a very abstracted form, but instead became the actual purpose of the painting."[11] The real "truth in painting," Mitchell seems to be saying, is the truth-in-painting, the shapes and, especially in Joan Mitchell's case, the colors that the painter finds in the canvas rather than in nature. Nature is there, to be sure, just as Cézanne is there, but it has been placed back inside the mind of the artist where it should be, and so freed from any referent other than itself. But it would be a mistake to think that this lack of any external reference means that the paintings are less unified or coherent than Cézanne's more referential approach. Indeed, they are perhaps more coherent in that the painter cannot, in this case, rely on any external point of reference. Instead, the "meaning" of Beauvais is colored meaning, plain and simple.

Harold Rosenberg famously coined the term "Action Painting" to refer to this immersion in the painting itself as opposed to referencing any external, representational content, but to understand better the particular "action" of this and other Mitchell paintings we must also approach them synaesthetically. By this I don't mean the actual synaesthesia that would, for example, hear the music of these works, although writers on Joan Mitchell have often noted her love of music—which, like Georgia O'Keeffe, she listened to while painting—and the particular influence of local bebop jazz on the New York School of the 1950s.[12] Rather, it is the "softer synaesthesia"—"tasting art," as opposed to eating it—in which the image produces meaning before it has separated the meaning from the image. In the left panel of *Beauvais,* the black strokes in the upper-half of the painting, with their occasional brown overlays, create a Miró-like calligram that "speaks" to the viewer like the subject of a sentence from a long-forgotten tongue. Their very opposites are the yellows relegated to the outer portions of the work, leading, in perfect consistency, to the orange of the bottom half and the green at the top. This carefully constructed composition (Joan Mitchell worked slowly, struggling over every stroke) is thus as much writing as landscape, word as image, but what it says is, literally, "in living color."

Nonetheless, there is a particular power in the blue here and elsewhere in Joan Mitchell's works. Mitchell's blue is distinctive, and so not to be confused with that of other painters who have shown a similar proclivity, such as Picasso during his so-called "Blue Period" or Chagall throughout his oeuvre. Indeed, Joan Mitchell's "ultra-marine" blue, if that is what it is, holds a very special place throughout her oeuvre and should probably have a name all its own ("Joan Mitchell Blue?"). Although the broad black brush strokes just discussed float atop, as it were, these paintings, it is the blues that somehow dominate. It is as if they are the chromatic center of the work even when, as here, they are not as dominant as they are in so many of Joan Mitchell's paintings. This is no accident, any more than it is an accident that blue dominates in the neurological references to synaesthesia and, of course, in music, where "the blues" are not only their own genre but, as in the case of the (supposedly) synesthete Duke Ellington, for whom "a D note looked like dark **blue** burlap while a G was light **blue** satin,"[13] a dominant reference throughout the medium (e.g., Gershwin's "Rhapsody in Blue").

Another way to describe *Beauvais* would be to apply the notion of "space/time synaesthesia." Since space cannot exist without its opposite, time, and vice versa, we might rightly conclude that our customary way of viewing the two separately is only secondarily related to the primordial unity existing between the two. This is the same unity as that between word and image, where paintings such as those of Paul Klee return us to the primordial unity between a word which *is* an image, as opposed to their usual separation between the word *and* the image. Klee's "hieroglyphs," and Mitchell's "calligraphy," are neither word nor image but both; in Mitchell's case, the brush strokes of *Beauvais* are language, but language that is synaesthetically imagistic, and colored at that. Similarly, time in *Beauvais* merges with the space that is reabsorbed back into time, as opposed to a more classical orientation in which time is frozen, and supposedly separate from space.

Sandro Parmiggiani talks about Joan Mitchell, following Duchamps and Maria da Silva, with "a common insight: space and time coincide in their formation, in such a way that acquiring the sense of space and discerning the meaning of time are parallel paths and processes which continually *cross over*; to explore space in a painting is also to revisit time" (p. 52, italics mine). Ordinary consciousness cannot understand what understanding, by its very nature, prevents it from understanding, namely, its own self-contestation, its own doubling as always already separate from its own positing of itself. This, I would argue, explains the curious nature of a diptych that is really one painting. The painting is double the way synaesthetic crossovers are double in creating a unity between two things that, like space and time, like the two parts of the painting, are really one. To look at *Beauvais* as the unity between two separate parts that are not really separate is to understand the synaesthetic beauty of a masterpiece that is, like every synaesthetic experience, greater than its parts.

Blue Tree (1964)

Figure 9.2

If art, as I have claimed, is "synaesthesia for the rest of us," Mitchell's *Blue Tree*, from her "middle period," is an excellent case in point. One clue to the synaesthetic properties of Mitchell's tree is to be found in this characteristic sketch of a tree by van Gogh.

Figure 9.3

In replacing the more traditional, objective representation of a tree with an almost hallucinogenic array of curved marks of different hues, van Gogh has not only enlivened the more realistic presentation. He has also made the tree move in the same way that van Gogh's other mature works move, and it is this movement that draws the viewer, like the artist, into the vortex of the work. But, since words-which-are-images, "écritures/peintures," has been discussed frequently in this work, one should also mention the calligraphic quality of these marks. This is a "language-tree," and the fact that there is no clear mark between the marks as tree and the marks as signifiers the painter has returned, just as Klee's "secret alphabet" returns, to the origin of language, thereby adding to the synaesthetic crossover where image and word "come together at the origin of each." Comparisons between van Gogh's and Mitchell's trees makes clear the importance of van Gogh on the entire abstract expressionist movement, but especially on Joan Mitchell. But that is not to say that van Gogh's is the only important influence on this painter, and on this painting.

Although she frequently eschewed the inevitable comparisons with Monet, despite—or perhaps because of—having once lived on property he once owned and whose famous gardens at Giverny were only a few miles from her home, it is impossible not to see the influence of Monet's later works on this painting. And yet, pressed up against the more naturalistic olive green, the blue of the tree wrests away any external referent and creates an explosion of color in the viewer that is more, not less, concrete than any objective representation. What I am referring to as the "quasi-synaesthetics" of this and other works is precisely this separation from objectivity—synaesthesia is by definition non-objective—in lieu of a "sensory crossover" in which metaphorical correspondences replace any "actual" reality. In this respect, we can invoke Baudelaire's notion that "Nature is a temple where living pillars/Let escape sometimes confused words," for what we are looking at here, *pace* many of Mitchell's critics, are not emotions per se but, rather, the world as it exists before emotions and other associations have been detached from things. That is why one must approach these paintings as calligraphy, for, if one does not, one risks losing the very meaning that the exceedingly careful construction of the work conveys.

Why blue? Why so much blue in these works, and, as mentioned, in so much else? Mitchell's blue is not really a natural color (there are no blue foods, although Alfred Hitchcock once famously served his dinner guests a meal of all-blue food for that very reason), and it is particularly not natural here. Whether or not Mitchell was an actual synesthete, her undeniable preference for the "power of blue" is related to the dominance of blue in actual synaesthesia. It invades these paintings, it takes them over in the same way that a synesthete sees a sound, or a number, as a particular color—it is the sound of a painting, and of a language, that one can only hear by seeing with "ears that truly hear," and hearing with "eyes that truly see."

No Birds (1988)

At the beginning of Alfred Hitchcock's epic film *The Birds* (1963) there is, even by Hitchcock's (and Saul Bass') high standards, an extraordinary title-sequence in which black, silhouette-like images of crows flash across the screen; there is no music here or, for that matter, anywhere in the film, with the only sounds here being those of the squawking birds (actually composed from electronic sounds). Freud would, of course, have much to say about this image of large "castrating" birds in setting the stage for a film about a grown man who still lives with his clinging, possessive mother.[14] I mention this here because of the long black horizontal lines of Joan Mitchell's own "epic" painting, her "remake" of van Gogh's "final" painting.

Figure 9.4

Figure 9.5

It has been said that Mitchell accepted the commonly held view of *Wheatfield with Crows* as van Gogh's final painting, and as representative of his death—a view she shared with Artaud, whose famous, turbulent essay on van Gogh Mitchell regarded as the best thing ever written about the painter. It is also worth noting that Mitchell painted her diptych version of van Gogh's double canvas[15] almost exactly one hundred years after van Gogh's death, a fact that would not have escaped the painter and would have only added to the artist's identification with the painting—Mitchell herself, who had been first diagnosed with cancer in the mid-eighties, was also not long for this world.

"No Birds?" The title of Joan Mitchell's painting, like those of many of her works, is playfully ambiguous. Similar to the futile exercise of trying not to think about something, the title belies itself in unavoidably referencing the very thing it is denying—in this case, the birds of van Gogh's late painting, which are present both in the black lines at the top of Joan Mitchell's painting (which is where they are in van Gogh's work) as well as in the reference to a painting in which there *are* birds. This is not to say, of course, that the artist is contradicting herself, for she clearly avoids any representation of any thing in this and any other of her "abstract" works. But it would also be a mistake to view Joan Mitchell's adaptation of one of her masters' works (it is, to return to the language of film, her only "remake") as not referencing van Gogh's birds. Indeed, if one were to be literal the painting would be better entitled "No Roads," because, while the birds are ambiguously present in the work, the famous three roads, and the central, oft-discussed "road to nowhere," are nowhere visible or even suggested. In "wiping out" the three roads Joan Mitchell seems to be saying that while she is clearly referencing the work of one of her masters, she is not referencing any object that can be found in van Gogh's painting, simply because such objective referents do not exist in Mitchell's work, however much they may be suggested.

Compared with other of Joan Mitchell's late paintings or, for that matter, her entire oeuvre, *No Birds* is fairly chaotic. Whereas, in the Cézanne-like *Beauvais* just discussed, there is a strong sense of impressionistic, or post-impressionistic, natural space, and a much stronger sense of composition, here there is a palpable sense of movement and excitement generated by the long horizontal strokes in the upper half and the more vertical but equally impassioned orange lines below. It is as if one is looking at a detail from another work rather than from the work itself. I am not suggesting that this painting is in any way inferior to Mitchell's others, but, rather, that Joan Mitchell seems to be channeling van Gogh's own sense of energy, and even accentuating it. In this regard Mitchell seems to have picked up on something that is often ignored in discussions of van Gogh's work, namely, that the wheat in van Gogh's painting, which is clearly referenced in Joan Mitchell's use of orange/yellow in the bottom half of her work, is bending in the wind, and the birds are, or course, also in motion.

It is often said that Joan Mitchell should be ranked among her colleagues of the New York School such as Franz Kline, a close friend of the painter's whose influence is clearly evident here and elsewhere in Joan Mitchell's work. *Rather, it should be said that Kline and others, such as Rothko and de Kooning, should be ranked with her*. For the use of Kline's signature black strokes is but a small part of the febrile activity of this work. And despite what was just said about the relative chaos of *No Birds*, there is still a great deal of composition in this unified work (this diptych is meant to coalesce, rather than those that are to remain "separate"), and the two main zones of black atop and orange below are accompanied by a number of "lesser" colors that are carefully balanced with the other, more dominant colors and which seem to have a life of their own. The pink blotches (as opposed to strokes), for example, add a distinctive depth to the canvas that creates a decidedly lighter mood.

And then there is the one bit of "Joan Mitchell Blue" in the lower left corner, one that is clearly meant to harmonize with one of the aforementioned pink blotches that rests atop it. Although relegated to this relatively small, "inferior" position, this small patch of blue replaces the artist's signature, attesting to the painter's ego-less world where colors such as this are directly felt, as opposed to the objects they represent.

Finally, one should also note the Joan Mitchell "drips." These are not, like Pollack's, part of the painting; they are clearly the "unfortunate" result of Joan Mitchell's habit of painting vertically. Nonetheless, they in no way detract from the painting because they aren't seen when one is looking correctly at the intended brush strokes. Mitchell clearly did not care about these, and nor should we, because if one feels the synaesthetic meaning of these lines and their colors, nothing else, particularly not a name or an object named, can exist. "No Birds," indeed.

10

Rock and Roll as Synaesthesia: Why Rock Lyrics (Don't) Matter

"Isn't perfect unity of text and music possible only when poet and composer are one and the same person? . . . I believe that music and word flow from the inspired poet and composer at the same *instant."*

(E. T. A Hoffmann)

Most writers on rock and roll music readily—or begrudgingly—admit that the lyrics aren't really poetry, at least not the kind that can stand on its own, without the music that accompanies it. (The recent outcry over Bob Dylan's being awarded the Nobel Prize for poetry is another example of this controversy.) For example, reviewing a book of Paul Muldoon's rock lyrics one writer notes: "*Like most rock lyrics, these seem thin apart from their music*—no careful admirer would mistake them for [Paul] Muldoon's strongest poems, though they nonetheless offer many pleasures."[1] If, one might wonder, the rock lyrics of a highly esteemed, Pulitzer Prize-winning poet can't stand on their own, whose can? Indeed, another example of this view of the questionable significance of rock's lyrics even found its way into the title of a review-essay of one of the staple books on rock lyrics: "*The Poetry of Rock: Song Lyrics are not Poems but the Words Still Matter*: Another Look at Richard Goldstein's Collection of Rock Lyrics."[2] And, finally, demonstrating a view that is closer to the explanation of rock lyrics offered here: "Though a study of song lyrics can provide much insight into the attitudes and philosophies of particular groups of people in particular places at particular times, and even help to shape discourses about culture at a broader level, to ignore the *sound* of pop and rock tracks is to do them a great disservice. The impact of these pieces fuses sound with ideas embodied in the words."[3]

Leaving aside the question of whether rock lyrics can stand on their own—they probably can't—let us take this latter view of the inseparability of rock lyrics from their context (and, indeed, from their recordings[4]) as a fact with which many critics and listeners would readily agree. But this view does not lead to the conclusion that many of those who agree with this proposition would assume, namely, that rock lyrics don't matter. Rather, I would like to propose a radically different view: *it is because the lyrics make MORE sense that they can't stand alone*. That is to say, the great rock song/lyric makes perfect sense when understood as an inseparable part of its music and of the performer who writes his or her own music and lyrics.[5]

What I am suggesting, then, is a position midway between the two prevalent views of rock lyrics, namely, that they matter a great deal and they matter not at all. While Bob Dylan can rightly say that "whatever I do . . . it's not in the lyrics,"[6] this does not preclude Dylan's own contradictory assertions about the value of his lyrics (as evident from his pleasure—however ambivalent—regarding the aforementioned award), leading to the inevitable conclusion that the lyrics matter greatly as unified with the music, and not at all when taken separately. In what follows I hope to demonstrate that this unity between word and music in rock and roll is based on the fact that rock and roll, like all great art, is inherently synaesthetic. As one of the great writers on synaesthesia and art and, particularly, the synaesthetic properties of music wrote: "Such is the power of music's spell that it grows ever stronger and can only burst the fetters of any other art."[7]

Chuck Berry: Hail Hail Rock and Roll!

Chuck Berry is a legendary musician whose distinctive guitar style has influenced virtually every rock and roll guitarist after him. And while his status as a lyricist is sometimes overlooked in lieu of his innovative instrumental prowess, this bias will actually help us to understand the relation of words to music in rock and roll, where even great lyrics such as those of Chuck Berry are inseparable from their total effect in the rock and roll recording. As noted in one of the numerous assessments of Berry's musical genius:

> Of all the early rockers, Chuck Berry was by far the most significant. He was really the first artist to exhibit many of the traits that would come to define the form. First, he featured his own electric guitar prominently in his music. He used the instrument to give his material a propulsive, driving rhythm underneath his vocals, and then used equally rhythmic lead parts to echo and accent his vocals. This presaged the overall importance of guitars and guitarists in the idiom. *Next, he exhibited the highest degree of musical integrity. Not only did he play guitar on all of his recordings, he wrote and sang all of his own material. The result is the most satisfying and consistent recorded canon of any of the early rockers. Others, like Buddy Holly and Elvis Presley, frequently relied on outside sources to supply their songs. The results were often uneven, with some of the best performances seeming to happen despite the supplied material, and not because of it.*[8] (italics mine)

Chuck Berry's *School Days* (1957) was one of Berry's earliest hits after the groundbreaking *Maybellene*, where Berry's fusion of rock with country a few years before (1955) had, according to many, virtually created what we now know as rock and roll. In addition to being one of "The Great Twenty-Eight," a compilation of all of Berry's pre-1965 Chess recordings, *School Days* stands out from those other hits as the first rock and roll anthem because of its final verses: "Hail, hail rock and roll/Deliver me from the days of old/Long live rock and roll/The beat of the drums, loud and bold."[9]

Our first indication of the synaesthetic unity between words and music in *School Days* is to be found in the song's first word, and in the first word of most of the subsequent stanzas: "Up," "Ring," "Drop," and "Hail." Berry uses these one-word beginnings to emphasize the highest, one-note beginnings of the musical verse. If the words were not written with the music, if the writer of the music was not the same as the writer of the words, the perfect unity between the two would not, in all likelihood, have been achieved. Berry heard the music and then came up with the perfect word or vice versa, although this is not to say that he could not have come up with different words than these (indeed, Berry rewrote the same song with different lyrics five years later as *No Particular Place to Go*). The song goes on to contrast the energy and excitement of the music, exemplified by the first word, with the boring drudgery of schoolwork. The youthful audience of rock and roll dictated Berry's high school reference, although the self-referential lyrics about rock and roll, as critics have noted, is a recurrent feature of other of Berry's lyrics (cf. *Johnny Be Good).* Indeed, the self-referential tendency in Berry's lyrics—referring, not to himself per se, but to the music that he is playing—is not uncommon in other rock lyrics as well, leading to the conclusion that the music is about the synaesthetic unity of music and lyrics—the powerful "Hail Hail Rock and Roll" in the climactic final stanza being a particularly good example of this.

School Days also reveals a pattern that is directly relevant to our thesis regarding the synaesthetic unity of rock music and lyrics. As mentioned, Berry is perhaps most famous for his distinctive guitar "licks," his way of playing lead guitar, which influenced virtually every subsequent rock guitarist. Those "licks" are amply evident here, and every line of verse is followed by a responsive guitar line. But there is more to this example of the inherent unity between music and lyric in rock and roll, for not only does a guitar line follow each verse line, but *Berry responds with his guitar musically to every verse in the same register as the preceding vocal line.* For example, in the first lines of each stanza which, as mentioned, begin with those one-word high notes mentioned earlier, Berry's guitar responds accordingly—corresponds—with a guitar line that is similarly in the highest register (using the highest strings). In subsequent lines of each stanza, lines that never regain such high pitches, Berry totally avoids using the high strings, using, instead, middle and lower strings that also correspond to the middle and lower registers of these subsequent lines. There are no exceptions to this pattern of *School Days,* which is all the more remarkable because it is highly unlikely that Berry was aware of this. This is further testament to the idea that rock and roll, as an original or, in the best sense of the word, primitive art form that had literally just burst onto the scene, is music which are lyrics which are "licks" that are all one *Gesamtkunstwerk,* one grand synaesthetic unity.[10] Indeed, Wagner himself "makes it clear that for him the setting of word to music is ultimately a product of the musicality of language itself . . . in other words, poetry is a kind of 'proto-music.'"[11]

Paul McCartney: *All My Loving*[12]

One of the very early, and still most recognizable, Beatles tunes, *All My Loving* was the first song that Paul McCartney composed by writing the lyrics first; as he told his friend and biographer Barry Miles, it was a departure from his and most musician/writers usual method of writing the music first, or the music and lyrics together.[13] That being said, the confluence of music and lyrics in this typically trite early Beatles lyric (cf. *I Want to Hold Your Hand*, *Love me Do*, all from the Beatles' first album in the United States, *Meet the Beatles*) is still representative of the synaesthetic unity of all great rock lyrics.

Hunter Davies' recent definitive book on *The Beatles' Lyrics*[14] gives the song surprisingly short shrift, and notes that "the words are fairly conventional, sending all his love to someone who is away, promising he will always be true, rhyming 'kissing' with 'missing,' 'you' and 'true.'" However, Davies goes on say that "it rings sincere and genuine. *It's the tune that really makes it*, the first four bars being especially haunting" (italics mine). Indeed, when applying a synaesthetic interpretation of the song (Davies' book does not interpret the words and music together as we are doing here), the first line of the first verse, "Close your eyes," which is composed of three descending notes, perfectly mirrors the closing of the eyes described by the lyrics, as does, to a lesser degree, the next rising line, which mirrors the kiss that is waiting. The next, third line, introduces the idea of longing and separation that is a staple of the Beatles, and of many rock lyrics that bemoan the separation of the oft-traveling musician from his home, and from his love. This too is reflected in the music, where "tomorrow" descends to "I'll miss you" which, instead of ascending like the preceding "I'll kiss you," reflects the sadness that accompanies this separation.

The next line of the first verse, "Remember I'll always be true," is an interesting departure from the preceding lines in moving from a major IV to a minor VI and then to a decidedly harsher, more dissonant major II to a major V. Rock's use of the major—as opposed to the minor—II is fairly common in blues and blues-inspired songs (cf. Ed and Lonnie Young's 1959 version of *Buy you a Chevrolet*—and its countless covers—or the Kinks' *You Really Got Me*—and its countless covers) but here it stands out for its bluesy harshness, a darkness that reflects the question of fidelity that is always implicit in such promises of fidelity. It has a threatening tone, and this is certainly in keeping with the fear of loss that is behind—but does not undercut—the promise of devotion that is the song's major—or is it minor?—intent.

The constant movement from major to minor (or, minor to major) chords, and the harshness of the "blues" chord just mentioned, syncs with the bittersweet sentiment of the lyrics, which continues in the second stanza with what Hunter Davies rightly refers to as the curious sexuality of this and other Beatles songs. (Like many of the early Beatles tunes, *All My Loving* follows the less typical verse/verse/chorus/chorus, versus verse/chorus/verse/chorus format.) Their early music, which is decidedly tamer than Chuck Berry's or Elvis' (and also why they seem closest to their namesake Buddy Holly and the *Crickets*, whose saccharine songs like "Words of Love"—which the Beatles covered—also avoided overt sexual references), is nonetheless very sexual but in a more repressed way. Here, there is a clear but disguised reference to masturbation in the first three lines: "I'll pretend that I'm kissing/The lips I am missing/And hope that my dreams will come true."[15] After this descent into Paul's dreamy reenactment of "kissing the lips" of his girlfriend the melody recovers after the ominous "blues" chord with the "rising from the ashes" of the last three lines, which declare—however unconvincingly—that he will attempt to resolve the problems of separation by writing, not occasionally, but "*every* day," and not with "some," but with "ALL my loving."

Indeed, the titular phrase "All My Loving" begins every line after the first two verses. "All my Loving," "All my Loving," "All my Loving" not only begins each new line but even, in the penultimate line, pushes aside any other words altogether. The lines are part of a different chord progression that make up the song's "chorus." The progression consists of a minor VI that has been a staple of this and many rock songs, but here it is followed by a downward suspension (actually an augmented C) in which a very dissonant C note is added to the C# minor—dissonant because of two half-tones in the same chord. This is not as complicated as it sounds, but it sounds complicated for it is midway, as it were, between a major and minor chord, which is what creates its distinctively + and – tone. This, combined with the major/minor chords that occur on either side of this suspended chord, highlight the entire song's reliance on the shift from major to minor chords and, more importantly, on the dissonant "blues"

II chords discussed above. These two dissonant chords are not only what make the song a great Beatles song, but they do so because the lyrics, too, as we have seen, are about a bitter-sweet romance that is suspended, quite literally, between both opposites, between presence and absence, faith and infidelity, devotion to another and masturbation, that is reflected in both the music and the lyrics.

There are two other (at least) aspects of the song that should also be approached synaesthetically. The first concerns George Harrison's jaunty, country-western-style guitar solo. There was a reason that Harrison's guitar of choice on this song and throughout the Beatles' early years was the Gretsch model named after Chet Atkins; it was a testament to the enormous influence of Atkins on Harrison—an influence that unfortunately suffered when the more blues-oriented style of Clapton, Beck, Hendrix, and others began to dominate the scene. Be that as it may, the jaunty, country-western solo (we recall Chuck Berry's country-western influences as well), which has only one, quickly passing minor chord, stands in relation to the rest of the song the same way that the major, brighter chords of the song stand in relation to the minor, dissonant ones. That is to say, the darker undertones of the song are clearly muted in the guitar solo, which thus stands in relation to the song "proper" as the more upbeat aspects of the song stand in relation to the less upbeat ones, a point that is emphasized even more when the song immediately goes back to the darker, minor-dissonant chords right after the solo, the end result being that the balance between major and minor, upbeat and sad, that dominates the rest of the song is ultimately denied in favor of the honky-tonk sentiment, a sentiment confirmed by the last, dominant major E chord. The Beatles, one might surmise, were not all that saddened by a separation that is contradicted by the very music that conveys it.

One of the most underrated aspects of Paul McCartney's illustrious career as a singer-songwriter is his brilliant bass playing, and that is nowhere more evident—which is saying a lot—than in this song. But is it really separate and distinct from the song itself? The way that the bass, at every turn, emphasizes the crucial minor and dissonant notes (that suspended C of the C# minor) suggests otherwise, but the "bottom line" is that the remarkable "walking bass line" that accompanies the verses—which is even more remarkable considering

McCartney's simultaneous vocals that are "walking" in a totally different direction—are as out of step with the melody as the triplets played by Lennon's rhythm guitar, with the end result being that McCartney and the other Beatles have literally walked away from the very separation they bemoan in the song's lyrics, a contradiction that, as we have seen, does not contradict but is the very essence of the song itself, and of the Beatles as a musical phenomenon. It is not really necessary to point to all the ways that the history of the Beatles, of their music and their lives, confirms the joyous sadness that is their legacy, and their synaesthetic indifference to all such separation. "All my Loving" thus refers to a totality of love that embraces everything, including its own separation from love. The wonderful over-dubbed, double-track vocals of the last verse, in which Paul's separation is belied by his unity with himself, confirms just that.

Tom Petty: *American Girl*[16]

> Q. What was the first great song you wrote?
> A. "American Girl." I thought, "I've set a bar for myself." Lyrically I had done something. I didn't know exactly what, but I realized I may have the potential to do this after all. And I thank [producer] Denny Cordell for the way he educated me . . . Denny drove home lyrics—that when you put a little truth in a song, it elevates things. And I remember him telling me, "Good singing is when you believe the singer." That's good, since I don't have a conventional voice.[17]

Like many American rockers, the late great Tom Petty pointed to the Beatles' 1964 Ed Sullivan performance as pivotal in his decision to pursue a musical career. It is perhaps surprising that the proudly southern Petty acknowledged the Beatles and other British bands as having had more influence on him in those early years than, say, Elvis. But what is not surprising is that the Beatles' influence on Petty had as much to do with their song-writing prowess as anything else (Elvis did not write his own songs).

One of the ways a synaesthetic interpretation of rock lyrics helps to solve the problem of whether "rock lyrics matter" is by joining the two together rather than either separating the lyrics entirely or ignoring them entirely.

(Printed lyrics of these songs inevitably err in their placement of certain words with the wrong lines and lines with the wrong stanzas.) As one recent writer on the subject pointed out, if rock lyrics really don't matter, why are they so necessary? (Rock instrumentals are a relatively rare part of the genre.) And, if they do matter, how do they matter? In joining the words and music of *American Girl* together one notices, first of all, something that a mere reading of the words would never discover, namely, that, in the first verse of *American Girl* Petty emphasizes certain words over others (to make this pattern clearer I have used a bold font for the words that are emphasized by the singer-songwriter):

> Well, she was an *American* girl
> Raised on *promises*;
> She couldn't help *thinkin'* that there was a
> Little more to life, *somewhere* else.

This continues throughout the song, and is most evident in the chorus, where each word is emphasized. The reason this is important for our purposes, and more than just a common, if subtle vocal technique, is that the emphasized words are the most important in terms of both the music and the ideas of the song and, as such, demonstrate the importance of keeping the words together with the music and its performance, as opposed to reading the words as they are usually printed out, as though each counted the same as all the others. The reason singer-songwriters don't do this when they write down the lyrics is that, in writing both together, this "goes without saying" or, one might say, "goes without singing." My point in drawing attention to this pattern, which is only evident in listening to the actual recording, is to emphasize that the words and the music are not separate or separable, and that there is music in the way, for example, the word "American," dominates both the music and the meaning of the first line.

Every other word of the first line is one syllable, yielding in importance to the 4-syllable "American" which dominates the line as it does the song. The musical AND verbal emphasis of this term—the only 4-syllable word in the song, with Petty adding a little extra to the beat of each syllable—is important in shifting the emphasis away from the girl—important for a number of reasons: first, because the song seems less about a girl than about Petty himself, and less about her dreams than about the "American dream" as it applies to everyone. The "girl" in question is dreaming of escape from her small town in Florida (whereby the reference to Highway 441), which is exactly what Petty did after growing up in Gainesville and dreaming of being a rock and roll star, despite all the odds against him. Indeed, it's hard to imagine that the concluding lines of the last verse "God it's so painful when something that's so close/Is still so far out of reach"—a line that musically draws out the "far" to emphasize the idea of distance—does not refer to Petty himself. Second, because Petty avoids the sexism of related songs like "American Woman" and "California Girls" by refusing to objectify women the way that those more blatantly commercial songs did.[18] (The disturbing use of the song in Demme's *Silence of the Lambs* is not an exception but, rather, proof of Petty's contempt for such commercialism.)

"After all it was a great big world": the syncopated triplets, which are repeated in A-*mer-i-can* girl and, even more distinctly, in the musical break that occurs after the second chorus as well as in the longer instrumental section that follows, epitomizes the lyrical/musical genius that Petty said he realized after writing this early song. It is, after all, a "great big world," and the musical emphasis confirms this. It also confirms the idea just discussed that the song isn't really just about a girl or just about America, for the world referred to is bigger than either, just as the rock song we are listening to, with its synaesthetic genius, is an "American song" reaching listeners all around the "great big world." We know, then, the nature of the obscure "one little promise she was gonna keep"; it is the fame that awaits those lucky enough to lay everything on the line to achieve it.

"Oh yeah, all right": Petty learned from the Beatles that "yeahs" (as in *She Loves You*) and "all rights" are not really words per se (there is no real "signified" to either of these in this context), but a reminder that words, whether "pure signifiers" like these or words that mean something, are never more important than their synaesthetic unity with the music. Similarly, the next two lines ("Take it easy baby/Make it last all night"), while they have seemingly no relation to the rest of the song, are in perfect harmony with the music: "Take it easy" slows the line while the more staccato "make it last all night" speeds it up, which serves as a reminder that all "rock and roll" is ultimately about the alternating rhythms of sex—the rest be damned!

Finally, the possibility of hearing "un-American" in addition to "an American" is consistent with the negative critique of the "American dream" that is also plainly evident in the lyrics and, indeed, in much of Petty's music and statements, which is not to say that he is un-American, but that the true American is not the gingoistic flag waver but the rebel, the refugee, the dissenter who "won't back down."

Gino and the Romantics: *What I Like about You*[19]

Given the stellar list of artists discussed thus far, this may seem an odd choice to include in this chapter on the synaesthesia of rock lyrics. One might have expected, for example, an analysis of one of the Rolling Stones' classics, like "Gimme Shelter," "Brown Sugar," or some such. And, I must confess, that was my original intention, but then something interesting happened. In listening to those tunes I realized that the division between words and music is greater than I would have liked in order to demonstrate the sort of synaesthesia that is my goal here, and this is doubtless due to the fact that the song-writing duo of Keith Richards and Mick Jagger works differently than the duo of, say, Lennon and McCartney, where the Beatles' divided their "library" of classics by distinguishing each other's songs according to which of the two mostly wrote—and then sang—the songs and lyrics. As I listened to the Rolling Stones' songs just mentioned I realized that their different approach lessened the unity between music and lyrics that I am arguing for here. This can vary, of course, from song to song depending on its particular genesis, but the synthesis in question is still, I would argue, less effective in this respect (and in this respect only).

The Romantics were—and still are—a punk-influenced rock band that came out of Detroit in the late 1970s. They are one of a number of "power" bands that emerged from the "motor city" (one thinks, in particular, of their predecessor Mitch Ryder), but who include among their various influences the "punk," "new wave" music that had emerged in Britain a few years before this classic recording. For all of its crudeness, and for all of the other aspects that add to its lesser status (e.g., the band never achieved the fame that the song itself can claim), this is a perfect example of the synthesis of rock music and lyric—perhaps it is an even better example because of these so-called deficiencies. Like The Knack's *My Sharona*, or Stevie Winwood's early *Gimme Some Lovin* (with the Spencer Davis Group), this is one of a very select group of rock songs that epitomizes the genre's dynamic appeal, and so it is a valuable example of how this appeal requires fusion, rather than separation, between words and lyrics.

The song begins without any lyrics per se. After two repetitions of the signature solo guitar chords that seem to set the song in the key of A (the first is punctuated by four claps), the rest of the band enters with one loud drum-accentuated "hey," when the song moves down to the key of E where, like a host of other rock songs, particularly in the "cruder" punk-influenced compositions, the song repeats the I-IV-II-IV unchanged to the end. (There is, however, a departure from this in the song's chordal solo.) This pattern, which continues into both the A and B "verses" and "chorus," begins with a rock and rolling back and forth between the aforementioned "hey" and then, in the same place in the measure (the last beat), "uh huh huh." These sounds are no more nor less meaningful than the (supposedly) more articulate words that follow. Indeed, the titular "What I like about you" that begins the first verse begins seamlessly from the previous "Hey" "Uh huh huh" of the intro. This is important, because the "sensical" and the nonsensical merge perfectly, thus demonstrating that, in a perfect rock and roll song like this one, the meaning of the words is not really meaning per se but, rather, a synaesthetic music-meaning.

And yet, one might protest, the lyrics of the first verse do make sense. Indeed, they do, but only as part of the music that carries them. Each word of the first and most important line is emphasized: What-I-Like-about-You, with the final "You" expressing the closeness of not only the singer and the person he is addressing but, more importantly, the closeness of the words—in that case the simple second person pronoun—and the music. In other words, the use, in so many rock lyrics, of such simple pronouns is a way of emphasizing that the words don't really matter as such but only as a way of connecting with the music, something that would be less direct if the words were less specific and/or meant more than merely perfect placeholders for the music. When Gino emphasized "YOU," and, in the next line, the memorably twangy, surprisingly two-syllable "tight" (also used later in "night"), holding the singer tight, or, later, keeping the singer warm at night, this is hardly poetry per se—indeed, it is not only inept ("thanks for keeping me warm at night honey"!) but, even worse, an extremely impoverished cliché. But the words are perfect when combined with the music (e.g., the "tight" expression of the word "tight," etc.); indeed, one would be just as foolish to rewrite the words to this classic rock song as one would be to elevate them to some kind of poetry per se. Rather, "it's true, that's what I like about you": the truth of the song is that "I like you" as confirmed, not by the words, but by the words and music together . . . "that's what I like about you!" Imperfect words make perfect sense when used in a rock song where the perfection is not in the music by itself (the reason instrumental rock music has always been far less successful) nor the words, but both. "That's what I like about you!"

Epilogue: Cole Porter: *Night and Day*

The thesis of this chapter, that rock and roll lyrics matter more, not less, because they cannot stand alone but are, instead, part of a synaesthetic unity that is characteristic of all great art, can also be argued negatively by pointing to the countless classic pop songs and jazz "standards" whose words were written separately by a different lyricist. (It is possible, of course, for a lyricist to write words that *do* fit music written by someone else, and for a single writer/composer to write words that do *not* fit their own music, but these are exceptions that do not disprove the rule that, artistically, the words and music must fit together synaesthetically.) A classic like "I can't give you anything but love" by Jimmy McHugh (music) and Dorothy Fields (lyrics), as wonderful as it is in so many other ways, is a good example of how an otherwise great song can still be deficient in marrying words and music together. The words, in this case those of a typical depression-era complaint about much love but little money, bear no relation to the jaunty tune which, unlike the Beatles song analyzed earlier, introduces not even one minor chord.[20] This is true of virtually all the pop songs from a genre, and from an era, when it was the exception rather than the rule for the same person to write both words and music together.

Such an exception, and, indeed, a very notable one at that, is Cole Porter, who was not only an enormously gifted musician but one of the very few composers of tunes for Broadway who wrote both words and music. Perhaps this is why his songs transcended their original shows, but it is definitely why these songs are now heralded as among the very best examples of their genre, and why not only accomplished jazz performers but many others, including many prominent rock musicians, literally "sing the praises" of his works by continuing to perform and record them.

As opposed to a song like the aforementioned "I can't give you anything but love," or other "standards" like "Sweet Georgia Brown," no one would argue that the words and music of "Night and Day" don't match up perfectly. Unlike those and other such standards, the listener is immediately aware, and continues to be so throughout the tune, that the "burning and yearning" sensuality of the words is aptly expressed in the exotic melody and chordal structure of the song itself. Beginning with the intriguingly odd dissonance of major 7th "A" note sung over a Bb chord, the entire song repeats the signature gesture of uniting differences. Night and day, desire and its fulfillment, "you" and "I," etc. are all separate but united in this typically (for Porter) elegant but candid expression of love and desire. The frequent use of Maj7 chords, beginning with the opening lines, represents the bright (as opposed to a flattened 7 or the minor 7 chords which follow) and yet exotic fulfillment of both opposing forces, and actually unites the opening two chords, separated only by a half-note, as well as that of the extraordinary half-note dissonance of the Bb sung over the A just mentioned. Indeed, Porter's use of such half-note dissonances and half-step chord progressions (Bb-A, G#min7-Gmin7, F#min7-Fdim7) throughout most of the song (the B section also utilizes this pattern by climbing up and down by half-chords) all combine to express perfectly the resolution of a dissonant longing that finds its fulfillment in dissonance, not without it.

The "B" section of "Night and Day" continues this emphasis on half-steps, and its relation to (un)fulfilled longing, with ascending and descending Maj 7 chords: D/D#/E/F, F/E/D#/D: "Night and day/Under the hide of me/There's a hunger burning and yearning/Deep inside of me." The inner/outer dichotomy referred to here is also referred to elsewhere in the song (e.g., "In the noisy traffic boom/In the silence of my lonely room"), and represents, again, a spatial equivalency to the temporal one of joining "you" and "I," "night and day." Again, the half-steps here, as well as the Maj 7 chords, the minor 7 chords' half-step progression, all represent this musically by minimizing, as much as possible, the separation between self and other, inside and outside, day and night, etc. And, finally, if the close proximity of all these opposites is also a correlate to the more sensual aspects of love—its goal of intercourse—it is not surprising that Porter refers to this when he says: "My torments won't be through/Until you let me spend my life making love to you/Day and Night/Night and Day." Underlying all the various forms of synaesthesia is a desired unity that, as we have maintained throughout this treatise, has its origin in the same desire for "oneness" that is the defining characteristic of human sexuality.

11

Hearing Images: Movie Music

Reading through the burgeoning corpus of academic and technical writings in the field, one rather simple fact emerges from the many controversies[1] surrounding "movie music": the best movie music is a perfect marriage between the visuals of the film (its "story") and its musical "accompaniment." The music, in those cases, does not distract from the story, or vice versa, which is why such music, however great, does not stand alone as music any more than, as we just saw, rock lyrics stand alone as poetry. The notion of a Wagnerian *Gesamtkunstwerk*, or a synaesthetic "total art work,"[2] in which two separate artistic media merge as one without ceasing to be two is not merely a theoretical ideal but the very touchstone of what makes for great movie music. As Max Steiner, the composer of many classic Hollywood film scores, bluntly states (and film composers, perhaps because of their marginalized status, are unusually forthright[3]): "I've always tried to subordinate myself to the picture. A lot of composers make the mistake of thinking that the film is a platform for showing how clever they are. This is not the place for it."[4] Our reason for focusing on this challenging genre in a work dealing with the relation of art to synaesthesia should be obvious: movie music, like all great art, is inherently synaesthetic as a place where sight and sound, as two separate sensory experiences, merge as one.

We will begin this chapter by examining Nietzsche's theory of "visual music" in *The Birth of Tragedy* in order to understand better the juxtaposition that is at work in this synaesthetic approach to movie music, and then, in the second part of this chapter, we'll focus on one example in particular, that of John Williams' score for *Close Encounters of the Third Kind* (*CE3K*). Although Williams' status as one of the great composers for film—he has now scored over 100 movies!—is well known, I choose this example rather arbitrarily, for there are almost as many examples of great movie music as there are great movies—indeed, if our thesis is correct, how could there not be?

* * *

"The problem of cinema music finds a Nietzschean solution, rather than Eisenstein's Hegelian one."[5] What Deleuze is referring to as a Nietzschean as opposed to Hegelian solution to the "problem of cinema music" is the former's less rational, less dialectical theory in which the Apollonian image emerges—is "born"—from the Dionysian musical matrix. As Deleuze puts it:

> In tragedy, the musical immediate image is like the core of fire which is surrounded by Apollonian visual images, and cannot do without their procession. In the case of cinema, which is first of all a visual art, it will be music which will be thought to add the immediate image to mediate images which represented the whole indirectly. (p. 239)

Although Deleuze—as well as Nietzsche—insists upon reversing the usual hierarchy and privileging music over the "story," this, like so many of Nietzsche's celebrated "*Umwertungen*," can be taken as an attempt to level the playing field in which, traditionally, the visual/objective realm is privileged over the auditory one. Although I suspect that there are many film composers who would prefer Nietzsche's more radical position, and many film directors who would sympathize with Quentin Tarantino when he states: "I immediately try to find out what would be the right song to be the opening credit sequence even before I write the script,"[6] for our purposes it does not matter whether one sees film music and story as one or whether one privileges, in order to reverse the usual tyranny of images, music over the story, as long as one does not privilege the story over the music and thereby lose their synaesthetic unity. Although one wouldn't expect Tarantino and Friedrich Schiller to agree about much, Schiller (as quoted by Nietzsche) said much the same thing as Tarantino with regard to his own compositional habits: "A certain musical disposition of mind comes first, and after follows the poetical idea."[7]

This notion, that reverses the usual order of things in which we think of music as an accompaniment to the story, informs Nietzsche's many references to the relationship between music and story in *The Birth of Tragedy*. While this is, of course, part of Nietzsche's celebrated goal of "reversing all values," the difficulties of understanding this particular reversal should not be underestimated, for it is, among other things, understanding itself that must be re-understood. Whether he is talking about lyric poetry such as that of Archilochus, or tragic drama such as that of Sophocles, or opera such as that of Wagner, or so-called "program music" such as that of Beethoven's 6th Symphony ("The Pastoral"), the words that accompany all these works do not so much follow the music as emanate—are "born"—from their musical matrix:

> [In such art] we find, moreover, the most intense effort of language to imitate the condition of music. . . . We have noticed again and again how a Beethoven symphony compels hearers to use pictorial speech . . . [although these descriptions] might appear rather checkered, fantastic, even contradictory. . . . But once we study this discharge of music through images in a youthful milieu, among a people whose linguistic creativity is unimpaired, we can form some idea of how strophic folk song must have arisen. . . . And when he [the lyric poet] looks at himself through that medium he will discover his own image in a state of turmoil: his own willing and desiring, his groans and jubilations, will all appear to him *as a similitude* by which music is interpreted. [Such art] is dependent on the spirit of music to the same degree that music itself, in its absolute sovereignty, is independent of either image or concept, that it may tolerate both. *The poet cannot tell us anything that was not already contained, with a most universal validity, in such music as prompted him to his* figurative discourse. . . . *Whenever it engages in the imitation of music language remains in purely superficial contact with it, and no amount of poetic eloquence will carry us a step close to the essential secret of that art.* (Section VI, 43–6, italics mine)

Art should not so much "aspire to the condition of music" (Pater) as it should be "inspired *by* the condition of music"; that is, it should exist *after* music, never before it. What Nietzsche is describing can, I believe, be understood best in syn-aesthetic, versus aesthetic terms, for "such art is dependent on the spirit of music to the same degree that music itself, in its absolute sovereignty, is independent of either image or concept, that it may tolerate both." That is to say, the image in a great painting, the story in a great play or movie, is a "figure," a metaphor, trope, "parable" or "similitude" (*Gleichnis*) as opposed to anything literal or objectively true, and, as such, is not what it is per se. In a word: *all great art is already music even when it does not involve music per se*, and, as such, is synaesthetic in joining, and not merely relating, music to any image or story that might emerge from it.

The example of American blues music is instructive in this regard, for blues music, as every true listener or practitioner knows, is not really "about" (unless one interprets this preposition spatially) the lyrics which, like every Greek tragedy, describe the destruction of the singer's or hero's mortal aspirations. Rather, the pessimistic—indeed, nihilistic—lyrics are only figuratively related to a musical essence that is, following Nietzsche, itself not even figuratively related to the lyrics. If blues lyrics such as those of Robert Johnson, Muddy Waters, Buddy Guy, and others, are like the storylines of Greek tragedy in being pessimistic and even nihilistic,[8] that is because such music involves what Nietzsche refers to as "strong pessimism," which ecstatically embraces the fullness of life and so must also embrace the worst that life has to offer. But this does not mean that the music is about the lyrics, which Nietzsche has carefully described as emerging from the music rather than, as our Socratic, scientifically minded objective way of thinking dictates, mistakenly privileging words and their objects over the music. Blues music, then, is synaesthetically related to its lyrics in producing words that express a musical essence that does not express them.

In a later section (XVI) of *The Birth of Tragedy* Nietzsche continues his insistence on music as the metaphysical "origin" of objects, stories and ideas: "In accordance with Schopenhauer's doctrine, we interpret music as the immediate language of the will, and our imaginations are stimulated to embody that immaterial world, which speaks to us with lively motion and yet remains invisible" (p. 101). And yet, we must guard against a possible misreading of this passage by recalling the discussion in Schopenhauer to which Nietzsche is here referring. Music is not a "direct expression of the will" if one understands Schopenhauer to mean our immediate subjective emotions; if that were the case, our animal friends would respond to Beethoven or the Beatles, which they clearly do not do (however much we would like to believe that they do). Rather, what Schopenhauer means by the will is the direct expression of our ideas, our thoughts, before they become ideas or thoughts as such (which is why animals do not hear music). Music, like all the arts for Schopenhauer, is an expression of the supersensible absolute as will[9] (and vice versa), not of the individual subjective will. It is for this reason that Schopenhauer, and Nietzsche after him, argued that words, stories, myths, etc. can be produced by, or otherwise correspond to, music:

> This close relation that music has to the true nature of things can also explain the fact that, when music suitable to any scene, action, event or environment is played, it seems to disclose to us its most secret meaning, and appears to be the most accurate and distinct commentary on it.[10]

"The true nature of things" refers to the metaphysical absolute, which music and art, according to Schopenhauer, express if they are true works of art. (In a later section—XXI—Nietzsche uses remarkably similar language to Schopenhauer's here: "Music . . . assures the spectator of a supreme delight . . . so that he is made to feel that *the very womb of things speaks audibly to him*" (p. 126).) In terms of synaesthesia, this means that the "oneness" which great art expresses is synaesthetic in unifying, in this case, music and story; neither is the secondary "accompaniment" of the other.

In this later section (XXI) of *The Birth of Tragedy* Nietzsche continues his radical reversal of the order of things by noting that the story—in this case the tragic *mythos*—is "a parable of those cosmic [sc. "metaphysical"] facts of which music alone can speak directly" (127). In other words, music "speaks directly" of an absolute which is then translated into a story that is only a parable of this "metaphysical" truth if it is severed from its musical essence. Nonmusical parables or other figures such as metaphor can only really be "understood" if they are heard musically, which is why we have had numerous occasions in this work to note the importance of metaphor's relation to synaesthesia. Metaphor, which always involves a synaesthetic, sensory crossover, is not really about its meaning but, rather, it is "about" its synaesthetic music. (This carries further recent, post-structuralist arguments discussed in Chapter 2 of this work that metaphor is always a "metaphor of metaphor" rather than a literal truth—"tenor"—of some kind.[11]) That this synaesthetic essence corresponds to what both Nietzsche and Schopenhauer refer to as the metaphysical absolute is made clear when Nietzsche derides those who think they can separate things from "things-in-themselves" in talking about a synaesthetic absolute that must deny this very separation: "About the contrast between the phenomenon and the thing-in-itself, . . . they [estheticians] have never learned anything nor, for some obscure reason, wanted to learn" (130). If, for Nietzsche and Schopenhauer, music is the essential truth to which the story must correspond (in the full Baudelairean sense discussed earlier), we can now understand more fully the oft-misunderstood notion of the Wagnerian *Gesamtkunstwerk* and apply it to movie music, which most writers on the subject agree evolved directly or indirectly from the Wagnerian idea.

Synaesthesia's Close Encounters

Bernard Herrmann once famously boasted that Hitchcock only made one-half of the seven films they collaborated on. This, to be sure, is an exaggeration (and one which effectively ended their work together), but it is less so when applied to the thirty films (and counting) Spielberg and Williams worked on together. Try as one might, it is impossible to imagine *Close Encounters of the Third Kind*, *ET*, *Indiana Jones*, *Jurassic Park*, and even *Schindler's List* without their music, or to imagine the music without their movies.

Although, as mentioned earlier, there are countless film scores to choose from as examples of great movie music, John Williams' score for *Close Encounters of the Third Kind* seems particularly apt as a finale to the present work. For *Close Encounters* is about a select group of individuals who possess extra-sensory abilities, which are either explicitly synaesthetic (the use of Kodály's visual symbols for music; the first "close encounter" in which "The sun . . . sang to him," etc.) or "quasi-synaesthetic" in unifying different senses, such as in Roy Neary's (Richard Dreyfuss) persistent visions of Devil's Tower or, more importantly for our purposes, in Williams' "visual music." That both forms of synaesthesia are at work here is evident when Claude Lacombe (played by Francois Truffaut in a directorial nod to the two directors' obsession with infantile consciousness) asks Roy Neary, in order to determine how he is able to know what the "aliens" are thinking, "Mr. Neary, are you an artist?" *CE3K*, I would argue, is less about aliens than it is about the alien experience of synaesthesia's own "close encounters," an experience which, in this film, is demonstrated not only in the film's storyline but in the synthesis between John Williams' musical score and Steven Spielberg's visual genius.

To watch any of the thirty or so films Steven Spielberg and John Williams made together is to enter a true *Gesamtkunstwerk* where music is an integral part of the total, synaesthetic experience. The films are in a way "reverse operas" in which the music will occasionally pause to allow the dialogue or visuals to assert themselves unaccompanied. But, in the case of *Close Encounters* and other Spielberg/Williams collaborations, the synthesis is even more complete than in Wagner, for in the movies the music cannot stand alone any more than the film can without the music (which is why recent attempts to recreate movie music in the concert hall is an unfortunate matter of economics, not aesthetics). Indeed, the synthesis is so complete that, as Williams and other great film composers have noted, the music is often never even noticed. As we argued in the case of great rock lyrics, great film music is incapable of standing alone not because it is inferior music (or, in the case of rock lyrics, poetry), but because it is in total, synaesthetic "sync" with the film for which it is scored. Although it is always tempting to try to divide the total, synaesthetic experience into its objectively recognizable components, to do so is to lose the "close encounter" of an artistic, syn-aesthetic experience in which the visual and the aural merge, much as they do with the famous five notes (and colors) of the musical hand signals used to communicate with the movie's "aliens."

If there is a visual equivalent to the five-note "communication theme" just mentioned it is surely the large mound of "stuff" which Neary first sees in a handful of shaving cream, then in a pile of mashed potatoes, and, finally, in the rock formation in Wyoming known as "Devil's Tower".

Figure 11.1

Ignoring the geological explanation for this remarkable structure, what strikes one most powerfully is its seemingly man-made nature. Not only the extraordinary vertical striations, but the entire mound seems to merge the human and the inhuman, man and inchoate nature, much as Heidegger described the Greek temple as seeming to emerge from the ground itself.

> Standing there, the building rests on the rocky ground. This resting of the work draws up out of the rock the mystery of that rock's clumsy yet spontaneous support. . . . The temple-work, standing there, opens up a world and at the same time sets this world back again on earth, which itself only thus emerges as native ground.[12]

Figure 11.2

The "tower" is natural, but it is also eerily *super*-natural in merging the human with what is beyond the human, which is doubtless why the aliens chose this spot for their climactic "close encounter" but, more importantly, why Spiel*berg* chose this to represent the creative process, a process in which something emerges from elsewhere to communicate with our synaesthetic origins. The rock formation is, in this respect, the same as the five-note "communication theme," for both are rather shapeless forms (Spielberg specifically asked for a nonmusical phrase for the theme, like a doorbell) to represent our origin, our "*Ur-sprung*," rather than something we know already. The rock emerges from the earth without, however, leaving the mystery of that origin behind, just as synaesthesia and art are reminders of an original unity between ourselves and the earth, and between our different senses.

In discussions of artistic synaesthesia, art works that explicitly rather than implicitly conjoin the senses, much attention has been given to artists like the Whitneys, Jordan Belson, Jim Hodges, Stan Brakhage, Brian Eno, and others,[13] who created works that explicitly attempt to unify light, music, and color. One artist in particular, Oskar Fischinger, should be mentioned here because of his "day job" at Disney where he worked on *Fantasia*, an extremely important film among works that are explicitly synaesthetic, and one that Spielberg has acknowledged as an important influence (along with Disney's *Pinocchio*, which is also referred to throughout *CE3K*). Not only does the climactic scene in which the lights of the alien craft move in correspondence with the music in a way that closely resembles many of the experiments in "visual music" just mentioned, but throughout the film the bulk of the "close encounters" with the aliens themselves are similarly synaesthetic. One remembers the early scene in which the aliens cause the toys in the little boy Barry's room to come alive and the record player to begin to play as examples of the aliens' power to merge the different senses. But most importantly in this regard one must note the "light shows" of the aliens' various crafts. "Light shows," which were most popular at the same time as Spielberg's coming of age as a director, were one of the ways in which many serious visual artists attempted to define their images musically. In *Close Encounters of the Third Kind* more attention is given to the dazzling displays of the aliens' ships than to the aliens themselves, perhaps because the real "close encounter" here is with the "dreamy arrays of colors that both extended the hallucinogenic state of the spectators and evoked synaesthetic responses [to] the pulsating light, whirring motors, and pounding rhythms. . . . The light show represented the culmination of what had started with Kandinsky some sixty years before."[14]

"Testing . . . one, two, three . . . Gentlemen, Ladies, take your positions please . . . could we have the lights in the arena down . . . we now show uncorrelated targets approaching from the north northwest." As a handful of stars separate from the night sky and begin to move toward Devil's Tower the music begins; indeed, the entire setup is less that of a scientific study than a concert which is about to begin, and in which music, in conjunction with light and images, is an integral part. As said in the Introduction to this treatise, "word and image" is to be replaced by "word *as* image," and by word/image *as* music.

To communicate with aliens, one must do so synaesthetically. Just as the music can't function without the lights accompanying it, the lights of the movie can't function without the music. Just as sound/music (the 5-note communication theme) cannot function by itself to make the necessary connection without their visual correlate (each note corresponds to a different color), so too Spielberg's film—or films—cannot function by themselves without their musical accompaniment.

There are in fact two "climaxes" to this encounter. The first ends when the ship finally responds to the communication theme—which it does, incidentally, with low-pitched orchestral bassoons that are not at all disguised as such, thereby driving home the idea that this is less an actual alien encounter than an artistic, synaesthetic one *à la Fantasia*. The first ship leaves to a round of applause and congratulations from the ecstatic scientists, who don't yet realize that the final "close encounter" has yet to occur. Before the "mother ship" finally lands a huge cloud formation gathers above the Tower.

Figure 11.3

While seemingly unnecessary, the clouds clearly resemble the Tower to emphasize the unity between these natural elements and, more importantly, between the earth and the sky, between our earthly selves and our less material, aetherial thoughts and ideas. This, in turn, explains the strange comment that Roy Neary makes to Lecomte after they have seen the mother ship land, when the scientist asks him what he wants. "I just want to know this is really happening." That is odd because, first of all, he is surrounded by hundreds of scientists who have seen, and are seeing, the same thing he is. Second, it is odd because we know that Lecomte is really asking him if he wants to join the select team of scientists who will be leaving with the aliens. Neary's reply *does* make sense, however, as a reference to the disbelief one must feel when confronted with an experience that confounds the normal separation of the senses and the normal sense of reality that relies upon them—indeed, it is the question "real" synaesthetes often ask themselves when first confronted with their unusual experiences. Neary is the only one who actually boards the ship because he, unlike the others, is in the grips of this un-reality, which is why the infantile aliens choose him and ignore the others. It is this moment, precisely, when we get the first musical reference to Pinocchio in the orchestral allusion to "When You Wish upon a Star," an allusion which again reminds us that *Close Encounters* is less about alien encounters than it is about the human, infantile, synaesthetic imagination.

A more ominous note is struck in the musical finale when Williams "changes his tune" by alluding a half-dozen or so times to the *Dies Irae* theme. This famous theme has been invoked in countless other films, including *Vertigo* and *Fantasia*, as well as by Berlioz (in the famously synaesthetic **Symphonie** *Fantastique*) and numerous other classical composers. But its presence here, in the carefully crafted finale (unlike many other composers, Williams' musical finales end exactly in sync with the final credit), is a bit of a mystery. *Dare we explain this final anomaly as an inversion of the communication theme, which it closely resembles*? If so, then we can understand this musical reference to the apocalypse as Williams' deep understanding of Spielberg's consistent vision of a world which, in departing from our normal vision of things, is necessarily as disturbing as it is delightful. In the words of Rilke, the "beginning of the beautiful is terrifying," because the beautiful is never just what it is, but is always also synaesthetically other. The mountain that the aliens chose for their visit is significant in many ways, some of which we have discussed already. But it is also significant in embodying this conjunction of joy and terror evident in the famous Bald Mountain sequence in *Fantasia*; for the actual name of this famous mountain is, in fact, *Devil's Tower*.

* * *

Addendum: On Eisenstein and the Associative Theory of Movie Music

In a recent essay published in a leading journal of movie music entitled "Modal Interchange and Semantic Resonance in Themes by John Williams: a semiotic examination of contemporary media music,"[15] Tom Schneller utilized what I would refer to as an "associative" model of movie music, one in which the emotive response to a number of different film scores is understood as the result of associations with earlier film scores and other compositions as well as with inherent associations between certain modes and chordal progressions and their respective affective responses.[16] The notion that different modes—say, the lydian, phyrygian, doric, etc—elicit consistently different responses is, of course, as old as music itself or, at least, as old as writings about music, beginning (in our Western tradition) with the Greeks. In order to clarify the value of this new synaesthetic model of art in general, and movie music in particular, it will help to compare it with this other, more traditional view.

The reader will have noted that, contained in the "associative" view of movie music just described are actually two different modes of association. The first, whereby film scores utilize previous music in order to elicit the same affective response (most famously, the use of Copeland in later westerns and in other celebrations of "Americana") need not claim any inherent connection between the music and its defined response, only that of a connection between the primary and later or secondary work. This leads to a sort of "chicken/egg" question as to whether the emotion is elicited by the music itself or by its association with the emotion elicited by the original work. The second mode of association does away with this confusion and simply declares an inherent link between the music itself and the emotion elicited. In other words, if Copeland's *Fanfare for the Common Man* is consistently used to describe certain kinds of people or situations it is not only because it was originally connected with those but, rather, because the music itself inevitably leads to these sorts of feelings and corresponding people and/or situations. In Schneller's self-avowed "semiotic" essay, with that methodology's view of an underlying system of preexisting cultural/linguistic meaning, it is clear that the former approach, namely, that the association is more a matter of "nurture" than "nature," of "langue" over "parole" (de Sausurre), dominates the discussion.[17]

And it is precisely here, in the dichotomy between a view of movie music as culturally determined—like language itself, which is, of course, the basis of semiotics—or "naturally" engendered, that the synaesthetic approach can be useful. Since Schneller's own approach does not close the door on an inherent connection between certain sounds and certain images, but merely ignores it, it is necessary to return to this question of origin, especially given the obvious importance of the notion of originality as long deemed essential to every work of art. (Something about which everyone from Telemachus in Homer's *Odyssey* to Heidegger all agree.) Although it is more than fair to note, as do Schneller and many others, that John Williams' use in *Jaws* of "the pounding, polytonal 'Augurs' chord [is derived] from Stravinsky's *Rite of Spring*, which Williams seems at first glance to have lifted wholesale" (p. 67), such "lifting" ignores the fact that Williams' originality—which Schneller and others acknowledge—is in marrying perfectly the polytonal chord with Spielberg's movie. Just as in Paul Klee's famous *écritures/peintures* (paintings which look like letters but are not), the key is in the original unity between word and image or, in the case of movie music, sound and image.

Thus, the problem with what I am referring to as the "associative" theory of film music is its failure to acknowledge that the basis for any successful association is the *original* synaesthetic unity between the film and its score. The writer's discussion of the bVII-I, or bVI-bVII-I progressions also helps to understand this difference:

> ♭VI–♭VII–I, in particular, has become something of a cliché in Hollywood music. Ron Sadoff describes the progression, which borrows the submediant and subtonic from the Aeolian mode, as a "portal of cultural affect" which elicits "hope, righteousness, and euphoria"—connotations that may in part derive from its prominent use in the influential Hollywood epics Ben Hur and Exodus. More recently, it has become associated with both movie studio logos (the Universal themes by James Horner and Jerry Goldsmith) and video game music (Super Mario Bros, The Legend of Zelda: Ocarina of Time). Since the mid-1960s, the progression has also been a mainstay of rock: "With a Little Help from my Friends" (The Beatles), "Lola" (The Kinks), "Crazy Little Thing Called Love" (Queen), to name a few. In the context of Williams' music, ♭VI–♭VII–I often assumes an implicitly or explicitly patriotic character. In the "Superman Fanfare," the progression is linked, through an archetypal figure of pop mythology, with "Truth, Justice, and the American Way . . . it conveys a sense of supercharged optimism which recalls not only the "big-country modalism" of Western scores and the pomp of 1950s biblical epics, but also the power progressions of rock with their connotations of blue-collar grit—in particular, Jimi Hendrix's famous rendition of the Star-Spangled Banner at Woodstock in 1969 which established ♭VI–♭VII–I as a concluding flourish for the national anthem. 61

Given the fact that Hendrix' use of the progression at Woodstock was drenched in irony whereas its use in Williams' score is not, one might wonder how useful it is to refer to it as eliciting "Family" and "Home" or "hope, righteousness, and euphoria." While, to be fair, the author recognizes that different nuances can be evoked in different contexts of the "same" mode or progression,[18] our notion of an original, synaesthetic unity between the film and its score demonstrates that such commonalities and allusions are of secondary importance.

Finally, in order to further clarify this synaesthetic approach to movie/music we can turn to one of the founding figures of cinema and one of its greatest theorists, Sergei Eisenstein. Eisenstein is, of course, commonly associated with his notion of montage, but, as most film scholars and all Eisenstein scholars readily admit, that term is far richer and more complex than its usual textbook definition would imply. In a recent essay collected in a volume of scholarly studies on *Sound, Speech Music in Soviet and Post-Soviet Cinema*,[19] Joan Neuberger reminds us of this while also demonstrating its relevance to synaesthesia:

> That synthetic unity, which he called the "montage image," contained an abstract understanding of the subject at hand that derives from the process of joining disparate elements: "Montage counterpoint as a form seems to correspond to that fascinating stage of the evolution of consciousness, when both preceding stages have been overcome, and the universe, dissected by analyses, is recreated once again into a single whole, revives by means of connections and interactions of separate parts, and appears as an excited perception of the fullness of the world perceived synthetically. . . . Mainly, it is necessary that everything, beginning from the actor's performance and ending with the play of the folds of his clothes, be equally immersed in the sound of that single, increasingly defined emotion that lies at the basis of the polyphony of a whole multifaceted composition." *"Nonindifferent Nature,"* quoted in "The Music of Landscape," p. 213

"The key phrase here," writes Neuberger, is the "sound of . . . emotion," *a more traditional use of the concept of synaesthesia understood as an involuntary neurological condition that activates multiple senses when only one sense is stimulated.*" But Eisenstein goes even further in identifying this primitive level of consciousness with synaesthesia, and the latter with its relevance to film/music. In an article he wrote concerning his famous collaborations with Prokofiev, Eisenstein calls this form of synaesthesia "the emotional visual and semantic sensation of the event" (*emotsional'no-obraznoe i smyslovoe oshchushchenie*) (p. 214), and, as we have also argued here, looked to art as the means to recapture this earlier state of consciousness ("Eisenstein saw a direct connection between the visual arts and this prelogical state" p. 214). In his discussion of Prokofiev he explains how this is possible:

> Prokofiev has the ability to "hear" in sounds the plastic visual depiction, [which] makes it possible for him to construct amazing aural equivalents of the visual depictions that fall in his field of vision. . . . In this particular sense, Prokofiev's music is surprisingly plastic, nowhere remaining mere illustration, but everywhere sparkling with jubilant figuration [*torzhestvuiushchei obraznost'iu*]; it reveals in amazing ways the internal movement of a phenomenon and its dynamic structure, which embody the emotion and meaning of the event. E, "P-R-K-F-V" . . . Reflecting here on the success of Ivan's score, Eisenstein writes in the same synaesthetic terms he finds so satisfying in the multisensory film. His specific examples are also wonderfully multisensory. p. 216

Although Eisenstein did not only imply but also explicitly defined art and, in particular, the relationship between sound and cinema in synaesthetic terms,[20] he shied away from identifying the actual neurological condition from its artistic embodiments: "Eisenstein points out that in poets and artists it is strongly present, however not usually beyond normal limits. He explains how these normal limits paradoxically provide a richer and more diverse subtlety of thought than is possible in extreme cases of synaesthesia."[21] Indeed, Eisenstein

> was wary of artists who attempted to consciously use synaesthesia, like Scriabin, who created equivalences between notes/keys and colors, attempted to blend smells with sounds, etc. He saw it as dangerously "megalomaniacal," (p. 144)

Added to the inherent paradox of synaesthesia is the further paradox of Eisenstein's emphasis on its importance and, at the same time, denial of its importance. But this, it turns out, is the kind of healthy paradox that is a sign of truth, not of logical incorrectness. Like movie music itself, art recreates an original unity—or, one might say, montage—that can never be defined in the sort of logical terms that fall apart as soon motion enters the picture—something the Platonic tradition, in its denunciation of art and Heraclitus, knew all too well in forever changing the relationship between art and truth.

Forever?

Epilogue:
Tasting Art: Art as Synaesthetic

Hegel once said that one can't write a proper preface to a book without explaining everything in the book and therefore contradicting what a preface should be.[1] Although an epilogue is somewhat less paradoxical, a certain contradiction remains, namely, that an epilogue is usually not written "after" the book but, rather, as part of it, more or less.

In this epilogue I wish to take up again an issue that arose many times in the writing of this work, namely, that of the relationship between "real" synaesthesia and what I have referred to throughout this work as its aesthetic counterpart. I have even gone so far as to argue that the term "aesthetic" be replaced with "synaesthetic," so strongly do I believe that this connection holds out the promise of a deeper understanding of the inherent mystery of art, also acknowledged by Hegel as discussed in the Introduction to this work. While I have referred to this "debate" numerous times in this work, in this epilogue I would like to address it somewhat differently in taking a step back from the work itself as well as by referring to one of the many examples of resistance to this idea that I have encountered while writing the present book.

In following the common practice of "testing the waters" of a new book by submitting one of its chapters to a relevant journal, I sent the previous chapter on movie music to an established journal devoted to that very subject. As it turned out, I chanced upon an editor who was himself involved in the neurological study of synaesthesia. An interesting exchange of emails between the two of us ensued, in which the editor argued in fairly strong terms that my essay was vitiated by my use of the term to describe what was not, in reality, synaesthesia:

> What many who use the term apparently do not realize is that synaesthesia is actually a *technical term* in medical science, as I have indicated, so that's where it comes from, and it is really up to science to explicate its nature for that reason. Just how synaesthesia made its way from scientific discourse

> into the arts and humanities as a sort of "term of art" remains something of a mystery. . . . As you probably realize synaesthesia has been a sort of "buzz word" in the arts and humanities for quite a while. . . . The main question is whether you are using the term as it is used in literature and the arts or in psychology and neuroscience where it is studied as an aspect of perception. As I have said before what you are really talking about are *intersensory correspondences*—the so-called "unity of the senses"—rather than characteristic perceptual phenomena of synaesthesia such as color-hearing. One does not need to be a synesthete to experience such correspondences, nor smoke opium as Baudelaire evidently did when writing about them in his famous poem . . . the use of the word "synaesthesia" to describe such correspondences as you are writing about is something of a misnomer that somehow got perpetuated to a misunderstanding of what synaesthesia is, whereas he argued persuasively that the term "intersensory analogies" was more apt, and for good reason. So I'm not sure one needs to even invoke the term synaesthesia in this connection, even though there is confusion about that in the literature. The neural mechanism responsible for experiences such as color-hearing is probably something above and beyond ordinary intersensory relationships.

In light of Daria Martin's recent work on "mirror-touch" synaesthesia in which she argues strongly against the general overemphasis on color synaesthesia, the editor's insistence on that one particular form of synaesthesia is telling. One might also take issue with the reference to Baudelaire's drug-induced experience of synaesthesia as normal. But the main issue in this *Auseinandersetzung* concerned my—and others'—use of the term at all. For my part, I explained to the editor in question that my claim was not that art is *synaesthesia* in the literal, neurological sense but, rather, that art is *synaesthetic*—that is, that art is inherently related to synaesthesia in numerous ways, beginning with what is commonly accepted as the all-important figurative nature of art. However, the editor adamantly refused to acknowledge any such middle ground in insisting that the term should not be applied to art at all.

Although one might wonder why a journal that concerns itself with movie music should be more interested in the scientific, as opposed to aesthetic, use of the term, in attempting to make my case I followed the editor's recommendation that I research Eisenstein's relevant comments on the subject (these are included in the chapter on movie music). I informed him that Eisenstein had himself adopted the same position that I held on the subject, namely, that real synaesthesia is not really relevant to art and is even detrimental to its proper functioning, *all the while insisting that art is nonetheless still synaesthetic.* Although my argument (and, I would add, that of Eisenstein and numerous other writers referred to in this book) was only for a relationship between the two synaesthesias, one in which the "scientific" phenomenon could help us to understand art in new and more concrete ways, the aforementioned editor—and he is by no means alone in this view—kept insisting that because art is not literally synaesthetic it could not be synaesthetic at all. This, even though, by the editor's own repeated admission, many writers, especially the "literature crowd" to which I supposedly belong, were all as benighted as I in our dogged insistence in using the term. Our correspondence ended with the editor admitting that he was on a sort of "one-person crusade" to stop not just me but everyone from using the term to refer to art. I will leave it to the reader to determine the validity of a position that claims to refute a contrary position that has already been conceded, namely, that art is not synaesthesia proper, and to decide, on the basis of this book and others, the validity of this middle ground.

The proof, as they say, is "in the pudding" or, in this case, in the chapters collected here that have tried to demonstrate, in many different ways and with reference to many different media, the relevance of "tasting" art in synaesthetic terms. As the philosopher Jean-Luc Nancy argued,[2] have we not missed something important in failing to listen to the many sensory crossovers that all art, and not just the Wagnerian "*Gesamtkunstwerk*," provides by unifying the various components that our ordinary way of viewing things maintains as discrete? In this respect, one might reply to the abovementioned editor and others who reject this notion in favor of literal synaesthesia and literal synaesthesia alone: "Aren't you mistakenly imposing scientific categories on the very thing that, as has been argued by Kant and numerous others,[3] denies any such strictly logical understanding?"

In the Introduction I referred to the possibility of future developments of this project, and, now that it is complete, I am even more convinced that we can and should deepen our understanding of this approach in general, theoretical terms as well as in specific, practical ones. With regard to the former, it is important to continue arguing for the "middle ground" between real synaesthesia and its aesthetic manifestations. But evidence for this can also be found by applying the notion of "syn-aesthetics" to more examples than those discussed here and to more media than those discussed here. For example, the art of acting, as mentioned in the Introduction, should be examined in light of the relatively new form of "mirroring synaesthesia"[4] in which the sensory crossover entails the leap from one's own personality to another's. Dance might be approached as a kind of "visual music" in which the movement of sound is transferred to the sound of movement, as it were. The tactile sense of sculpture was mentioned briefly in the chapter on Picasso's Vollard Suite, but perhaps even classical pieces like Bernini's might be better understood by approaching them with the same haptic sensibility as their more modern counterparts by Rodin, Maillol, Brancusi, Arp, and others. Similarly, our appreciation of classical paintings, such as those epitomized by Dutch artists of the seventeenth century, might be deepened by approaching them the way one hears the music of O'Keeffe and feels the texture of Picasso's cubism. Musically, the tone paintings of Rimsky-Korsakov (himself a reputed synaesthete), Debussy, Stravinsky, and, indeed, classical music in general, can be approached as transforming sound into something that is not really sound at all but, rather, the colored feelings of a thinking that listens to itself. Conversely, all art touches us with a music that is as visual as it is aural.

If all this seems decidedly metaphorical, recall that metaphor, itself, is the very basis of art's sensory crossovers. The difference, however, between the traditional notion of metaphor's importance to all the arts, beginning with Aristotle's insistence that metaphor is the "greatest element" in art,[5] and a synaesthetic as opposed to merely aesthetic approach, is that artistic metaphors and other sensory crossovers, are, like "real synaesthesia," themselves literal and not, as Aristotle also argued, merely analogous to a more fundamental, objective truth. Like the colored grapheme synaesthesia that insists upon the color of a particular number or letter, art, such as the colored letters of Paul Klee discussed earlier, insists upon the literal truth of its own logical fallacies and contradictions. When "words and images come together at the origin of each," there is no longer a separation between sound or image and sense, and vice versa. Sound, image, and other sensory phenomena *are* meaning, as opposed to merely *having* meaning:

> "O body swayed to music, O brightening glance,
> How can we know the dancer from the dance?"

The answer to this, as to many of Yeats' rhetorical questions, is, quite simply, that one cannot.

Notes

Chapter 1

1 Quoted by Phillipe Junod in "The New Paragone," *The Arts Entwined: Music and Painting in the Nineteenth Century*, eds. Morton and Schmunk (New York: Garland, 2000), p. 25.

2 Georg Wilhelm Friedrich Hegel, *Introductory Lectures on Aesthetics*, tr. Bernard Bosanquet (London: Penguin, 1993), p. 29.

3 Paul Gordon, *Art as the Absolute: Art's Relation to Metaphysics in Kant, Fichte, Schelling, Hegel and Schopenhauer* (New York/London: Bloomsbury Academic, 2015/17).

4 Dani Cavallaro, *Synaesthesia and the Arts* (McFarland & Company, Jefferson North Carolina, 2013), p. 44.

5 Although she does not discuss acting per se, in her recent, groundbreaking volume of essays on *Mirror-Touch Synaesthesia: Thresholds of Empathy With Art* Daria Martin discusses the recent movements toward interactive and performance, as well as "the question of art spectatorship, including an emphasis on attunement, intersubjectivity, and intercorporeality, based art" (p. 15), as based on synaesthetic mirroring.

6 See Junod, "The New Paragone."

7 Zelter in 1783, quoted in "*The Arts Entwined: Music and Painting in the Nineteenth Century*," p. 1.

8 "Like the Romantics, they [painters] believed paradoxically in the possibility of a Gesamtkunstwerk and an ideal of 'pure' music uncontaminated by the visual or literary arts." Marsha Morton, "From the Other Side," in *The Arts Entwined: Music and Painting in the Nineteenth Century*, eds. Morton and Schmunk (New York: Garland, 2000), p. 11.

9 In his understandable celebration of a certain purity that led him to embrace the formalism of cubism and other "abstract" forms of painting Greenberg was led to denounce more transformation forms of art and, indeed, the transformational,

synaesthetic properties of abstract art itself (see chapters on Picasso and Rouault included in this volume):

> Greenberg, we have seen, defined purity against such a point [art as absolute], so that only "by excluding from each art whatever is intelligible in the terms of any other sense . . . would non-musical arts attain 'purity' . . . "It is perhaps a little ironic that Greenberg sees modernism as an expression of modernity addressed to purity, and an attitude of static, detached contemplation." Simon Shaw-Miller, *Visible Deeds of Music* (New Haven: Yale, 2002), p. 146

10 "There is properly speaking but one Absolute work of art, which may indeed exist in altogether different versions, yet is still only one." F. W. J. Schelling, *System of Transcendental Idealism* (1800), tr. Heath (Charlottesville: University of Virginia Press, 1978), p. 231.

11 Morton, "From the Other Side."

12 Although Kant placed music as least among the arts, ironically, it is the best example of his new romantic aesthetic; cf. Carlyle, music "leads us to the edge of infinity," and Mme de Stael, "music awakens in us the sentiment of infinity," Morton, p. 5.

13 Wagner is opposed to "hybrid forms," "The New Paragone" Junod, "*The Arts Entwined*," pp. 32–3.

14 "Monet's work did not look musical." Kermit Champa, "Painted Responses to Music," in *The Arts Entwined: Music and Painting in the Nineteenth Century*, eds. Morton and Schmunk (New York: Garland, 2000), p. 107.

15 Junod, "The New Paragone," p. 27.

16 Richard E. Cytowic, "Synaesthesia: Phenomenology and Neuropsychology—A Review of Current Knowledge," in *Synaesthesia*, eds. Simon Baron-Cohen and John E. Harrison (Oxford: Blackwell Publishers, 1997), p. 21.

17 Cavallaro, *Synaesthesia and the Arts*.

18 E.g. Simon Shaw-Miller's *Visible Deeds of Music*, quoted in Nicolas Chare's *After Francis Bacon: Synaesthesia and Sex in Paint* (Ashgate, 2012), p. 114.

19 Baron-Cohen and Harrison (eds.), *Synaesthesia*.

20 In a short review of Nabokov's first novel *Mary* (Wall Street Journal, 7/30/2016) the author Marcel Theroux quotes the main character's remembrances of his first love: "'Mary,' Ganin repeated again, trying to put into those two syllables all the music they had once held—the wind, the humming of telegraph poles, the

happiness—together with another, secret sound which gave that word its very life."

21 In *Synaesthesia and the Arts* Dani Cavallaro also argues for this middle ground: "The analysis undertaken in the following pages will hopefully show that it is quite possible for a work to elicit cross-sensory responses in its recipients even if it is neither he product of an actual synesthete's creativeness, not a self-conscious attempt to simulate synaesthesia. . . . The reactions brought forth by a work of this kind are not genuine synaesthetic experiences. Nevertheless, they approximate synaesthesia." p.117

22 Baron-Cohen and Harrison (eds.), *Synaesthesia*, p. 109.

23 Cavallaro, *Synaesthesia and the Arts*, p. 80.

24 "This rhetorical position has scientific support. Broadly speaking, we all emerge from a synaesthetic ground. *There is strong evidence that human babies experience synaesthesia in the normal course of their development,* and that these early neural connections are later in life 'pruned' as brains develop." Daria Martin, *Mirror-Touch Synaesthesia: Thresholds of Empathy With Art* (Oxford: Oxford University Press, 2017), p. 10, underlining mine.

25 Marc-Jacques Maechler, who presented a paper at the Fifth International Conference on *Synaesthesia in Art and Science* (Alcala la Real, 2015) on "Implications if there are more synaesthetes than assumed." Dani Cavallaro confirms that "some researchers maintain that all human beings are initially synesthetes and only ceaseto be so when their brains relinquish unnecessary sensory linkages, whereas synesthetes retain the natural tendency to make such connections." *Synaesthesia and the Arts*, p. 5. Richard Cytowic (*The Man Who Tasted Shapes*, MIT Press, April, 2003, p. 166) also argues that synaesthesia is an ongoing, "unconscious" part of everyone. Cytowic's work is discussed at length by Cavallaro, *Synaesthesia and the Arts*, pp. 27–30.

26 "Grossenbacher and Lovelace . . . have explained the phenomenon in terms of disinhibited feedback." Cavallaro, *Synaesthesia and the Arts*, p. 25.

27 An argument also made by Sara Kofman in *The Childhood of Art: An Interpretation of Freud's Aesthetics*, tr. Woodhull (New York: Columbia University Press, 1988).

28 See Sigmund Freud, *The Interpretation of Dreams*, tr. Strachey (New York: Basic Books, 2010), where words are not "signifieds" but "signifiers" whose "meaning" is derived from [their] physical shape, sounds, connections to other words (condensation, displacement), etc.:

> Dreams, then, think predominantly in visual images—but not exclusively. . . . Nevertheless, what are truly characteristic of dreams are only those elements of their content which behave like images, which are more like perceptions, that is, than they are like mnemic presentations . . . we shall be in agreement with every authority on the subject in asserting that dreams hallucinate—that they replace thoughts by hallucinations." (p. 79)

29 There are many adherents, and some detractors, to this view of synaesthesia as part of our original, infantile consciousness. For example, with regarded to the theory (discussed by Baron-Cohen) of "Preserved Neural Connectivity":

> The normal adult human brain does not contain direct neural connections between auditory and visual areas. However, the early developing brain in many species does. This theory holds that, probably for genetic reasons, in individuals with synaesthesia pathways between auditory and visual areas in the brain continue to exist beyond neoteny. *Synaesthesia*, p. 110

Also, Richard Cytowic, while not rejecting this view, raises the interesting question of why children don't exhibit synaesthetic tendencies in greater numbers than their adult counterparts: "I had found no clinical evidence to support the hypothesis that synaesthesia might be more common in children, as authors from earlier eras claimed." Baron-Cohen, p. 33.

30 Martin, *Mirror-Touch Synaesthesia*, p. 10.

31 See Hegel's *Introduction to the Lectures on Fine Art* XXXV et ff. I discuss Hegel's argument in Gordon, *Art as the Absolute*, pp. 150–51.

32 "The Figure in the Carpet," in *Eight Tales from the Major Phase* (New York: Norton, 1969). James discusses his story in the Prefaces to Volume XV of The New York Edition of his works.

33 Iser's own analysis of the story is also given "In lieu of an Introduction" to his manifesto of "reader-response" criticism, *The Act of Reading* (Baltimore: Johns Hopkins University Press, 1978).

34 Those who would follow Iser in objecting to the seriousness of James' tale need only read—as apparently Iser did not—James' own comments on the novella in the aforementioned Preface to Volume XV of the New York Edition.

35 James' Preface makes clear that the story is about the proper way of interpreting art and literature in general, and not just Hugh Vereker's oeuvre:

> What I most remember of my proper process is the lively impulse, at the root of it, to reinstate analytic appreciation, by some ironic or fantastic stroke, so far as possible, in its virtually forfeited rights and dignities.

36 "The thingly element is so irremovably present in the art work that we are compelled rather to say conversely that the architectural work is in stone, the carving is in wood, the painting in color, the linguistic work in speech, the musical composition in sound." Martin Heidegger, "The Origin of the Work of Art," in *Poetry, Language, Thought* (tr. Hofstadter): *Der Ursprung des Kunstwerkes.* Derrida, *Memoirs of the Blind* (originally published as *Mémoires d'aveugle*, 1990) (New York: Harper and Row, 1971), p. 20.

37 This remarkable phrase, and its variants, which are referred to a number of times in this work, comes from J. Hillis Miller's discussion of Paul Klee's works, where "picture and word seem to come together at the origin of each":

> The same thing in another way can be said of those late paintings by Klee that represent rows of what seem to be either primitive drawings or letters in some unknown and as yet undeciphered alphabet. In these figures *picture and word seem to come together at the origin of both.* These strange signs are not yet either pictures or letters. They are the originating point where both coincided before their separation. p. 74

I discuss Miller's theory of *Illustration* in *Illustration of J. Hillis Miller*, a paper delivered at a conference celebrating Miller's works, and subsequently published in *Word and Image.*

38 There are, according to studies on the subject, at least eighty different forms of synaesthesia.

39 *The Science of Knowing: J.G. Fichte's 1804 Lectures on the Wissenschaftslehre* (Albany: State University of New York, 2005), pp. 120, 124, 158.

40 For example, in *The Beast in the Jungle*, where John Marcher also represents the exclusion of the rational, positivistic mind from its own unconscious.

41 See Derrida's two essays on metaphor—"White Mythology" and "The Retreat of Metaphor," discussed next in *Art as Synaesthesia.*

42 Quoted in Baron-Cohen, p. 87.

43 In addition to the well-known "Dream and Lie of Franco" etchings, there are numerous drawings of Franco in, for example, the Barcelona Picasso Museum which closely resemble this figure.

44 It is worth noting, in this regard, the importance Roland Barthes placed on connotation as artistic truth in *S/Z*.

45 According to quoted in Chare (*After Francis Bacon: Synaesthesia and Sex in Paint*) Bacon was "haunted" by Aeschylus' "The reek of human blood smiles out at me" (113).

Chapter 2

1 This the title of one of the revelatory works referred to in "*The Figure in the Carpet*," discussed in the Introduction.

2 Jacques Derrida, "White Mythology: Metaphor in the Text of Philosophy," tr. F. C. T. Moore, *New Literary History 6.1 On Metaphor* (Autumn, 1974): 5–74.

3 Cleanth Brooks, "The Language of Paradox," in *The Well-Wrought Urn* (New York: Houghton Mifflin, 1975).

4 This notion of doubling as it applies to metaphor and art in general is the subject of my first book, Paul Gordon, *The Critical Double: Figurative Meaning in Aesthetics Discourse* (Tuscaloosa/London: University of Alabama Press, 1995).

5 P. Ricoeur, *La métaphore vive* (Paris: Seuil, 1975).

6 Kerry Brougher and Olivia Mattis, *Visual Music: Synaesthesia in Art and Music since 1900* (The Museum of Contemporary Art, Los Angeles, 2005), p. 43.

7 Martin, *Mirror-Touch Synaesthesia*, p. 8. See Lawrence E. Marks, *The Unity of the Senses: Interrelations Among the Modalities* (New York, San Franscisco, and London: Academic Press, 1978), and "On colored-hearing synaesthesia: Cross-modal translations of sensory dimensions."

8 S. Kofman, *Nietzsche et la métaphore* (Paris: Galilée, 1985).

9 Nietzsche "Truth and Lies in an Extra-Moral Sense," Collected in *Philosophy and Truth*, tr. Breazeale (Atlantic Highlands: Humanities Press, 1979).

10 I discuss this poem, which is itself based on Kant's famous footnote about Isis in the third *Critique*, in Gordon, *Art as the Absolute*.

11 This is the model proposed in Gordon, *The Critical Double*.

12 J.-L. Nancy, *Listening*, tr. Charlotte Mandell (New York: Fordham University Press).

13 Derrida, "White Mythology."

14 Heidegger, "The Retrait of Metaphor," in *Psyche: Inventions of the Other*, eds. Peggy Kamuf and Elizabeth Rottenberg (Stanford: Stanford University Press, 2007), p. 63.

Chapter 3

1 Heidegger, "The Origin of the Work of Art."
2 Homer, *The Odyssey*, tr. Fitzgerald (New York: Vintage, 1990), p. 12.
3 "In the figures," says J. Hillis Miller of an *écriture/peinture* of Paul Klee, "picture and word seem to come together at the origin of both" *Illustration*, p. 74.
4 Gordon, *Art as the Absolute*.
5 There are a number of derisory readings of this passage, beginning with Meyer Shapiro's, to which Derrida (in *La vérité en peinture*) added his own.
6 Barbara Creed, *The Monstrous-Feminine* (New York: Routledge, 1993).
7 Hagi Kenaan, "Tracing Shadows: Reflections on the Origin of Painting," in *Pictorial Languages and Their Meanings*, Liber Amicorum in Honor of Nurith Kenaan-Kedar, eds. C. Versar and G. Fishof (Tel Aviv University Publishing, 2006).
8 "White Mythology," in *Margins of Philosophy*, tr. Alan Bass.
9 "Enough and more than enough has been said about painting. It may be suitable to append to these remarks something about the plastic art. It was through the service of that same earth that modeling portraits from clay was first invented by Butades, a potter from Sycion, at Corinth. He did this owing to his daughter, who was in love with a young man; and she, when he was going abroad, drew in outline on the wall the shadow of his face thrown by the lamp. Her father pressed clay on this and made a relief, which he hardened by exposure to fire with the rest of his pottery; and it is said that this likeness was preserved in the shrine of the Nymphs." Pliny, quoted by Kenaan, "Tracing Shadows," p. 20.
10 Chare, *After Francis Bacon: Synaesthesia and Sex in Paint*.
11 *Sein und Zeit*, #34, "Da-sein und Rede. Die Sprache," p. 163.
12 Christopher Fynsk, *Thought and Historicity* (Ithaca: Cornell University Press, 1986), p. 28.
13 Kaja Silverman reinforced the synaesthetic "acoustic mirror" of her earlier, landmark work on the role of women in film as part of cinema's non-logocentric epistemology with her later "turn" to Heidegger (Silverman herself refers to her discovery of Heidegger as a "major turning point in my life") in *World Spectators* (Palo Alto: Stanford University Press, 2000).
14 See *Introduction to Metaphysic* (1935), ch. 4, "The Restriction of Being": "We have to free ourselves from the opinion that *logos* and *legein* originally and

authentically mean thinking, understanding and reason" (130). It would be worth considering in this respect (although Heidegger does not do so here) the transformation of the one sense into the other in Plato, especially with regard to the Platonic idea of dialogue, as in the dialogue on friendship (the *Lysis*).

15 IM, p. 131.

16 IM, p. 141.

17 Martin Heidegger, *Der Satz vom Grund, Sechste Stunde* (Pfullingen: Neske, 1978); *The Principle of Reason, Sixth Session*, tr. Lilly (Bloomington: Indiana University Press, 1996).

18 There are, however, indications in Heidegger's earlier work of this notion of art as *aletheia*. For example, in the same section which contains the stating about *Dasein* as "hearing the voice of the friend" he states: "Die Mitteilung der existenzialen Möglichkeiten der Befindlichkeit, das heist das Erschliessen von Existenz, *kann eigenes Ziel der 'dichtenden' Rede werden*" (*S/Z*, p. 162, italics mine). After writing this qualifying footnote I found this reference to the same passage in a footnote to Nancy's essay on "La decision d'existence": "On ne s'interrogera pas plus, ici, sur ce privilege [sc. of poetic discourse], qui reste sans explication ni explicitation dans *Être et temps*" (p. 241).

19 *What Is Philosophy?*, quoted by Derrida, *L'oreille*, p. 368.

20 Jean-Luc Nancy, "La decision d'existence," in *Être et Temps de Heidegger*, p. 239. This passage about reading occurs on the same page as the aforementioned parenthetical passage on the reference to "hearing the voice of the friend." "The Decision of Existence," in *The Birth to Presence*, p. 92.

Chapter 4

1 "Yet, as the word's etymology indicates, synaesthesia is not restricted to the realm of the senses." Without referring to sensory concomitances per se, the poet calls upon another type of synaesthesia to convey his perception of dichotomous "others" that merge into a synthetic Je. For instance, in "L'Héautontimorouménos," which calls to mind Rimbaud's echo, "Je est un autre," Patrick Meadows, "Baudelaire's Syncretic Extensions of Synesthesia," *Symposium* 65.2 (2011): 117–133; 118.

2 In his work on the relation of music to the visual arts Simon Shaw-Miller notes that "synaesthesia is central to Baudelaire's aesthetic." *Visible Deeds of Music*, p. 52.

In another work dealing with the synaesthetic relation of the arts in the nineteenth century Marsha Morton writes:

> Nineteenth-century enthusiasm for synaesthesia began with E.T.A. Hoffmann, whose ideas gained additional recognition through the publicity of Baudelaire's writings. Hoffmann (who identified the hero of his story Kresleriana as the "little man in a coat the colour of C sharp minor with an E major coloured collar") inspired Baudelaire's poem Correspondences and was frequently cited by him. Synesthetic experiences described by Hoffmann in Kreisleriana haunted Baudelaire's aesthetic vision.... For Baudelaire [said] "what would be truly surprising would be to find that sound could not suggest colour, that colours could not evoke the idea of a melody." Junod, *The Arts Entwined*, p. 14.

3 See Patrick Labarthe, *Une poétique ambifuë: Les "corresponances,"* in *Les Fleurs du mal: Colloque de la Sorbonne.*

4 Ibid., p. 124.

5 Charles Minahen, "Correspondence Theory and the Case of Baudelaire's Sphinx Intertext," *Romance Quarterly* 39, no. 2 (1992).

6 Geoffrey Wagner, *Selected Poems of Charles Baudelaire* (New York: Grove Press, 1974).

7 See Baron-Cohen and Harrison (eds.), *Synaesthesia.*

8 Indeed, at an international conference on the subject held in the south of Spain I encountered some resistance from these actual synesthetes to my synaesthetic approach to all art, although some seemed satisfied with my distinction, between literal and artistic synaesthesia. I address this issue throughout this work as well in the epilogue.

9 "There is properly speaking but one absolute work of art, which may indeed exist in altogether different versions, yet is still only one." Schelling, *System of Transcendental Idealism* (1800). This notion is discussed throughout my previous book, Gordon, *Art as the Absolute.*

10 David P. Luke and Devin B. Terhune. "The Induction of Synaesthesia with Chemical Agents: A Systematic Review," *Frontiers in Psychol*ogy 4 (2013): 753.

11 See Martin on *Mirror-Touch Synaesthesia.*

12 Tr. Roy Campbell, *Poems of Baudelaire* (New York: Pantheon Books, 1952).

13 Roland Champagne, "The Devil's Advocate: Baudelaire's Cat as the Daimon of Erotic Mysticism in Les fleurs du mal," *The Romantic Review* 93.4 (2002): 434.

14 William Aggeler, *The Flowers of Evil* (Fresno, CA: Academy Library Guild, 1954).
15 Mario Richter, *Les Fleurs du mal* (Geneva: Slatkine, 2001), p. 213.
16 Aggeler, *The Flowers of Evil.*
17 S. Freud, "The Poet and Daydreaming," in *Collected Papers*, Vol. IV (London: Hogarth Press, 1956).
18 Jakobson, R. "Two Aspects of Language and Two Types of Aphasic Disturbances," in *On Language* (Cambridge: Harvard University Press, 1995).
19 Richter, *Les Fleurs du mal*, p. 213.
20 George Dillon and Edna St. Vincent Millay, *Flowers of Evil* (New York: Harper and Brothers, 1936).
21 This term was presented to me as an alternative to my synesthetic model. The problem with such associative models is that they deny the fundamental synaesthetic unity that is the basis for the association. See my discussion of this in the Addendum to my chapter on "Hearing Images: Movie Music" (Chapter 11).
22 In the chapter on Klee I discuss Freud's notion that when script (words, letter, numbers, etc.) appear in dreams they cease to function as referential but are their own material reality.
23 Labarthe, *Une poétique ambifuë: Les "corresponances,"* p. 125.
24 Aggeler, *The Flowers of Evil.*
25 Regarding the two preceding poems: "Or maintenant, nous entron dans la *réalité concrete de la vie*" (author's italics). Richter, *Les Fleurs du mal*, p. 208. Although Richter's analysis seems too "post-colonialist," his argument for seeing the moored "French" ships as comparable to his own "mooring" in the arms of his exotic lover is brilliant.

Chapter 5

1 Michel Foucault, *This Is Not a Pipe*, tr. Harkness (Berkeley: University of California, 1983), pp. 32–3.
2 Alejandro Vallega, "Paul Klee's Originary Painting," *Research in Phenomenology* 43 (2013): 463.
3 See ch. 1, fn. # 35.
4 Dennis Schmidt, *Between Word and Image* (Bloomington: Indiana University Press, 2013), p. 82.

5 "It is arguably in Klee's work that one encounters the most enthusiastic celebration of creative gestures capable of crossing dimensional and spatial barriers. . . . Klee's whole opus evinces syncretic proclivities that are in themselves redolent of synaesthesia" (Cavallero, p. 59).

6 Porter, Aichele, *Paul Klee's Pictorial Writing* (Cambridge: Cambridge University Press, 2002), p. 133.

7 Quoted by Aichele, *Paul Klee's Pictorial Writing*, p. 7.

8 Freud, *Interpretation of Dreams*, p. 88.

9 "Whereas graphemes generally determine color, phonemes tend to evoke synaesthetic tastes." Richard E. Cytowic and David M. Eagleman, *Wednesday is Indigo Blue: Discovering the Brain of Synaesthesia* (Cambridge: MIT Press, 2009), p. 37.

10 Cavallaro notes that dreams provide "a dimension in which humans renew their bond with their primordial synaesthetic substratum" (111).

11 See Paul de Man's discussion of this in "Sign and symbol in Hegel's Aesthetics," *Critical Inquiry* 8.4 (Summer, 1982): 761–75.

12 "Two Aspects of Language and Two Types of Aphasic Disturbances in Fundamentals of Language."

13 For more on Heidegger's appreciation of Klee, see Dennis Schmidt, op. cit.

14 Roland Barthes, *S/Z* (New York: Hill and Wang, 1974), p. 122.

15 Honoré Balzac, *The Unknown Masterpiece and other Stories* (New York: Dover Thrift Editions, 2013), pp. 3–6.

16 "Though we cannot *know* these objects as things-in-themselves, we must yet be in position at least to *think* them as things-in-themselves," p. 27.

17 "But the infinite finitely displayed is beauty." Schelling, *System of Transcendental Idealism* (1800), p. 112.

18 I share Simon Shaw-Miller's rejection of Greenberg's nonsynaesthetic interpretation of modern art in general and, in particular, of works by Klee that would "introduce elements that disrupt the purism of modernist thinking." *Visible Deeds of Music*, p. 122.

Chapter 6

1 Immanuel Kant, "Critique of Teleological Judgment," in *The Critique of Judgment*, tr. Meredith (Oxford: Clarendon Press, 1952), pp. 61, 66.

2 Schelling, *System of Transcendental Idealism* (1800), pp. 12, 218.

3 Greenberg's infamous but influential dismissal of Rouault is discussed in Georges Rouault, *Mystic Masque: Semblance and Reality in Georges Rouault*, ed. Schlosser (Chicago: University of Chicago Press, 2008), p. 426 et passim.

4 Rouault, *Mystic Masque (MM)*.

5 Kant, *The Critique of Judgment*, p. 179. See also Pierre Hadot, *The Veil of Isis* (Cambridge, 2006).

6 Jean-Luc Nancy, *The Ground of the Image* (New York: Fordham, 2005), p. 122.

7 "Rouault often gave a picture its own frame in which the contours, like the lead strips in the lancets of the church windows, have their beginning and end points. . . . The strong interweaving of individual elements of the painting with the frame brings about yet another intensification of the two-dimensional quality of the painting." Rouault, *Mystic Masque (MM)*, p. 383.

8 Kant, *The Critique of Judgment*, p. 68.

9 Rouault, *Mystic Masque (MM)*, p. 443.

10 Freud discusses at length the many taboos on touching, and offers a psychoanalytical interpretation of same, in Sigmund Freud, "*Totem and Taboo*," tr. Strachey (New York: Norton, 1950), "Taboo and Emotional Ambivalence."

Chapter 7

1 Francisco Seraller, *Picasso Vollard Suite* (Madrid: NP, 1993) p. 26.

2 "Little has been said about the almost ubiquitous presence of music and musical instruments in the work of the cubists." And, even in Picasso's pre-cubist works, "Nearly half between 12-14 include musical subjects." Shaw-Miller, *Visible Deeds of Music*, p. 90.

Chapter 8

1 *Art History News*, 7/17, 2012.

2 There seems to be some disagreement regarding the date, although I agree with the curator and O'Keeffe expert Barbara Buhler Lynes, that it is most likely the earlier. There is also some disagreement regarding the title; if I understand Ms.

Lynes explanations of the very complicated factors determining titles, Stieglitz labeled the painting on the back (O'Keeffe did not sign or title the rectos of her works after 1910) "Pink No 2," but the "first title," while not written on the verso, is widely attested and written, by O'Keeffe herself, on the catalogue of her works compiled at Abiquiu.

3 According to Heather Hole; see http://nellshawcohen.com/blog/2011/01/georgia-okeeffes-favorite-music/.

4 Brougher and Mattis, *Visual Music*, p. 59.

5 Quoted in Hunter Drohojowska-Philip's, *Full Bloom: The Art and Life of Georgia O'Keeffe* (New York: Norton, 2004), p. 130.

6 Brougher and Mattis, *Visual Music*, p. 35.

7 Quoted in Brougher and Mattis, *Visual Music*, p. 62.

8 Judith Zilczer, "Music for the Eyes: Abstract Painting and Light Art," in *Visual Music: Synaesthesia in Art and Music Since 1900*, ed. K. Brougher (London: Thames & Hudson, 2005), pp. 25–86.

9 "One should . . . choose events that are impossible but plausible in preference to ones that are possible but implausible." Aristotle, *Poetics*, tr. Else (Ann Arbor: University of Michigan, 1970), XXV.

10 Heidegger's famous ekphrasis on the Greek temple, in "The Origin of the Work of Art," is discussed in Chapter 3 of this work.

11 This line from *Being and Time* (*Sein und Zeit*, #34, "Da-sein und Rede. Die Sprache," p. 163) is discussed at length in Jacques Derrida's, *Les politiques de l'amitié, suivi de L'oreille de Heidegger* (Paris: Galilée, 1994) and in the final section of Chapter 3 of this work.

12 I discuss the stigma attached to female genitalia in "Revis(ion)ing Freud's Medusa," *Psychoanalysis, Culture & Society* 19 (March 20, 2014): 113–26.

13 Paul Rosenfeld, in 1921, quoted by Drohojowska-Philip, *Full Bloom*, p. 201.

14 Randall Griffin, *Georgia O'Keeffe* (New York: Phaidon, 2014).

15 Griffin, *Georgia O'Keefe. Part 3—Floral paintings and sexuality*, https://mydailyartdisplay.wordpress.com/2014/05/08/georgia-okeefe-part-3-floral-paintings-and-sexuality/ Posted on May 8, 2014.

16 O'Keeffe had works by Freud in her library of works at Abiquiu.

17 "It is worth remarking that the genitals themselves, the sight of which is always exciting, are nevertheless hardly ever judged to be beautiful . . ." *Civilization and Its Discontents*, tr. Riviere (New York: Dover, 1944), Section II, p. 16.

Chapter 9

1 Patricia Albers, *Joan Mitchell: Lady Painter* (New York: Alfred Knopf, 2011).

2 Bob Duggan, review of Albers' book, http://bigthink.com/Picture-This/did-joan-mitchell-have-the-finest-mind-in-modern-american-art.

3 "Van Gogh emphasized the abstract nature of color relationships by referring to them as pictorial 'symphonies' . . . [his] musical conception of color was an important factor in the development of his mature style" Morton, "From the Other Side," p. 13.

4 In these figures *picture and word seem to come together at the origin of both.* J. Hillis Miller, *Illustration* (Cambridge: Harvard University Press, 1992), p. 74.

5 Véronique Fóti, *Philosophy Today* 60.2 (Spring 2016): 397–405; 398.

6 Ref. "Adversity and Practices of Painting: Merleau-Ponty, Monet, and Joan Mitchell." Origin on form/content (or cut this clause).

7 Yvette Lee, "Beyond Life and Death: Joan Mitchell's Grande Vallée Suite," in *The Paintings of Joan Mitchell*, ed. Livingston (Berkeley: University of California Press, 2002), p. 68.

8 Fóti, *Philosophy Today*, p. 401.

9 Beauvais, 1986. Oil on canvas, diptych. 110.25 × 157.5 inches (280.04 × 400.05 cm). Private collection. © Estate of Joan Mitchell.

10 Ohlsen, ed., *Joan Mitchell* (Heidelberg: Kerher Verlag, 2008), p. 53.

11 Ohlsen, ed., *Joan Mitchell*, p. 20.

12 "Formal links between the bebop of Charlie Parker or Dizzy Gillespie and Abstract Expressionist painting are unmistakable and can hardly be seen as coincidental—if not deliberately intended—similarities." *Joan Mitchell*, ed. Ohlsen, p. 20.

13 http://pitchfork.com/thepitch/229-what-the-hell-is-synaesthesia-and-why-does-every-musician-seem-to-have-it/.

14 I discuss this and other films of Hitchcock in *Dial 'M' for Mother*.

15 These double-square canvases were only used by van Gogh him in June and July 1890.

Chapter 10

1 Reviewed in *Publisher's Weekly*, October 22, 2012; italics mine.

2 Peter Astor, *Popular Music*. Cf. also this title by Robert Christgau: *Rock Lyrics Are Poetry (Maybe)*.

3 John Encarnacao, "Musical Structure as Narrative in Rock," *Journal of Multidisciplinary International Studies*, 8.1 (January 01, 2011): 1.

4 Encarnacao rightly argues that one should speak of a recording rather than a song when referring to rock music, as a "cover" is not merely a different version, but a different aesthetic entity altogether: "The use of the term 'recording' is deliberate. The term 'song' is inadequate here, as songs may be found in various arrangements, performances and recordings, and each version may differ in respect to structure and instrumentation." p. 5.

5 It is interesting that the preponderance of great rock and roll songs are written by the performer or performers themselves, as opposed to the prevalent tendency in pop music for artists to perform others' lyrics. (Cf. songs such as Tina Turner's version of Elton John's/Bernie Taupin's *Tiny Dancer*, where the words have virtually no relation to the music) The former is obviously more "synaesthetic" insofar as the musician writes the words as he writes the music.

6 As Peter Astor notes (quoting an essay by Theodor Gracyk), p. 146.

7 E. T. A. Hoffman, *E.T.A. Hoffmann's Musical Writings*, ed. Charlton, tr. Clarke (Cambridge: Cambridge University Press, 1989), pp. 96–7.

8 http://www.reasontorock.com/artists/chuck_berry.html.

9 Listen to the original recording on YouTube: https://www.youtube.com/watch?v=DHG5-GxI_Es.

10 As Simon Shaw-Miller notes, the original inspiration for Wagner's Gesamtkunstwerk was the "multi-media" (involving song, dance and music) performances of Greek tragedy. *Visible Deeds of Music*, pp. 39–40.

11 Shaw-Miller, *Visible Deeds of Music*, p. 41.

12 Listen to the original recording on YouTube: https://www.youtube.com/watch?v=1OJHVZ7qhwI.

13 Barry Miles, *Paul McCartney: Many Years from Now* (New York: Henry Holt and Company, 1997), p. 148.

14 Hunter Davies, *The Beatles Lyrics* (Weidenfeld and Nicolson, London 2014), p. 49.

15 This was written before the recent revelation by McCartney of mutual masturbation sessions with Lennon et al.

16 Listen to the original recording on YouTube: https://www.youtube.com/watch?v=FyStwRYLzlI.

17 *Rolling Stone* interview with David Fricke, August 14, 2014, Issue 1215, pp. 44–66.

18 Despite Brian Wilson's genius, the Beach Boys were not really a rock band in the same vein as British and British-inspired bands (like The Heartbreakers), an

example being the use of studio musicians like "The Wrecking Crew" to record their songs.

19 For a video of the original band performing this classic, see https://www.youtube.com/watch?v=Rqnw5IfbZOU.

20 Ignoring that of the typical (in jazz) II–V progressions, which are, of course, not really minor (II) but major (V).

Chapter 11

1 Among these issues: the use original orchestral music versus pre-existent music, such as popular recordings; the use of synthesizers, and many subtler issues, such the use of "empathetic" versus "anempathetic" sound (sc. sound that works with or "against the grain" of the action).

2 Cavallaro (*Synaesthesia and the Arts*) refers to Wagner's "famous concept of the Gesamtkunstwerk . . . as the ultimate synthesis of all the arts under the aegis of music," p. 56.

3 E.g. Bernard Herrmann's statement, discussed later, about Hitchcock only making one-half their collaborations, and his (and other composers') routine dismissal of directors as musical imbeciles.

4 Mervyn Cooke, *A History of Film Music* (Cambridge: Cambridge University Press, 2008).

5 Gilles Deleuze, *Cinema II*, tr. Tomlinson/Galeta (Minneapolis: University of Minnesota Press, 1989), p. 239.

6 Cooke, *A History of Film Music*, p. 485.

7 Friedrich Nietzsche, *The Birth of Tragedy*, tr. Gollfing (Garden City: Doubleday, 1956), p. 37.

8 I discuss tragedy's relation to the blues, and vice versa, in Paul Gordon, *Rapturous Superabundance: Tragedy after Nietzsche* (Chicago: University of Illinois, 2001).

9 I defend this thesis in the book preceding this one, which is in a sense its logical precedent, Gordon, *Art as the Absolute*.

10 Arthur Schopenhauer, *The World as Will and Representation*, vol. 1, tr. Payne (New York: Dover, 1969), #52, p. 262.

11 For example, Derrida, "White Mythology."

12 In *Poetry, Language, Thought*, tr. Hofstadter (New York: Harper, 1967), p. 42.

13 See Kerry Brougher's essay on "Visual-Music Culture," in *Visual Music: Synaesthesia in Art and Music since 1900* (The Museum of Contemporary Art, Los Angeles, 2005), pp. 88–179.

14 Brougher, *Visual Music*, p. 170.

15 Tom Schneller, "Modal Interchange and Semantic Resonance in Themes by John Williams: A Semiotic Examination of Contemporary Media Music," *Journal of Film Music* 6.1 (2013): 49–74.

16 "Musical stereotypes cause stereotypical physiological reactions. These have not yet been systematised by physiologists, but composers intuitively employ certain devices which are suited to triggering specific reactions in the listener." Zofia Lissa, *Ästhetik der Filmmusik* (Berlin: Henschel, 1965), p. 355, quoted by Schneller, p. 49.

17 Although Schneller does not discuss his own self-described use of semiotics, this reliance on "nurture over nature" is evident throughout, as in this quote from Philip Tagg: "Filmgoers . . . perceiving time and time again similar combinations of visual, verbal, sonic, and musical message, have been taught set patterns of musical behavior through identification and reinforcement." p. 50.

18 At the end of his essay the author includes the usual academic nuance: "Musico-cinematic topoi, as Tobias Plebuch has noted, are not "fixed symbols like traffic signs," but flexible and constantly evolving signifiers that can be handled with subtlety: "Once a topos is established, a composer or improviser may just use a characteristic feature and inject, for example, a tiny but recognizable dose of mysterious, pastoral, religious, or military sound into any scene."

19 *Sound, Speech Music in Soviet and Post-Soviet* Cinema, ed. Koganovsky/Salazkina (Bloomington: Indiana University Press, 2014).

20 Robert Robertson, *Eisenstein on the Audiovisual: The Montage of Music, Image and Sound in Cinema* (London: Taurus, 2009). See, in particular, Chapter 4, "Synaesthesia."

21 Robertson, *Eisenstein on the Audiovisual*, p. 20.

Epilogue: Tasting Art: Art as Synaesthetic

1 "For whatever might appropriately be said about philosophy in a preface . . . none of this can be accepted as the way in which to expound philosophical truth." Georg Wilhelm Friedrich Hegel, "*The Phenomenology of Spirit*," tr. Miller (Oxford: Oxford University Press, 1977), p. 1.

2 "Is listening something of which philosophy is capable? Hasn't philosophy superimposed upon listening something else that might be more on the order of understanding?" Nancy, *Listening*, p. 1.

3 This is the subject of my previous book: Gordon, *Art as the Absolute*.

4 According to Martin (*Mirror-Touch Synaesthesia*), while the first case of synaesthesia was reported in 1812, the first case of "mirror-synaesthesia" was only reported in 2005.

5 "But by far the most important thing is to be good at metaphor. This is the only part of the job that cannot be learned from others; on the contrary it is a token of high native gifts, for making good metaphors depends on perceiving the likenesses in things." *Poetics* 22.

Bibliography

Aggeler, William. *The Flowers of Evil*, tr. William Aggeler (Fresno: Academy Library Guild, 1954).

Aichele, Porter. *Paul Klee's Pictorial Writing* (Cambridge: Cambridge University Press, 2002).

Albers, Patricia. *Joan Mitchell: Lady Painter* (New York: Alfred Knopf, 2011).

Aristotle. *Poetics*, tr. Gerald F. Else (Ann Arbor: University of Michigan, 1970).

Astor, Peter. *Popular Music* 29, No. 1 (January 01, 2010).

Balzac, Honoré. *The Unknown Masterpiece and Other Stories* (New York: Dover Thrift Editions, 2013).

Barthes, Roland. *S/Z* (New York: Hill and Wang, 1974).

Baudelaire, Charles. *Poems of Baudelaire*, tr. Roy Campbell (New York: Pantheon Books, 1952).

Brooks, Cleanth. "The Language of Paradox," in *The Well-Wrought Urn* (New York: Houghton Mifflin, 1975).

Brougher, Kerry. "Visual-Music Culture," in *Visual Music: Synaesthesia in Art and Music since 1900* (Los Angeles: The Museum of Contemporary Art, 2005).

Brougher, Kerry and Zilczer, Judith. *Visual Music: Synaesthesia in Art and Music since 1900* (Los Angeles: The Museum of Contemporary Art, 2005).

Cavallaro, Dani. *Synaesthesia and the Arts* (Jefferson: McFarland & Company, 2013).

Champa, Kermit. "Painted Responses to Music," in *The Arts Entwined: Music and Painting in the Nineteenth Century*, eds. Morton and Schmunk (New York: Garland, 2000).

Champagne, Roland. "The Devil's Advocate: Baudelaire's Cat as the Daimon of Erotic Mysticism in Les fleurs du mal," *The Romantic Review* 93, No. 4 (2002).

Chare, Nicolas. *After Francis Bacon: Synaesthesia and Sex in Paint* (Surrey: Ashgate, 2012).

Creed, Barbara. *The Monstrous-Feminine* (New York: Routledge, 1993).

Cytowic, Richard E. "Synaesthesia: Phenomenology and Neuropsychology—A Review of Current Knowledge," in *Synaesthesia*, eds. Simon Baron-Cohen and John E. Harrison (Oxford: Blackwell Publishers, 1997).

Cytowic, Richard E. and Eagleman, David M. *Wednesday Is Indigo Blue: Discovering the Brain of Synaesthesia* (Cambridge: MIT Press, 2009).

Davies, Hunter. *The Beatles Lyrics* (London: Weidenfeld and Nicolson, 2014).

De Man, Paul. "Sign and Symbol in Hegel's Aesthetics," *Critical Inquiry* 8, No. 4 (Summer, 1982): 761–75.

Deleuze, Gilles. *Cinema II*, tr. Tomlinson/Galeta (Minneapolis: University of Minnesota Press, 1989).

Derrida, Jacques. *Mémoires* (New York: Columbia University Press, 1986).

Derrida, Jacques. *Memoirs of the Blind* (Chicago: University of Chicago Press, 1993) (originally published as *Mémoires d'aveugle*, 1990).

Derrida, Jacques. *Les politiques de l'amitié, suivi de L'oreille de Heidegger* (Paris: Galilée, 1994).

Derrida, Jacques. "The Retrait of Metaphor," in *Psyche: Inventions of the Other*, eds. Peggy Kamuf and Elizabeth Rottenberg (Stanford: Stanford University Press, 2007), pp. 48–80.

Derrida, Jacques. "White Mythology: Metaphor in the Text of Philosophy," tr. F. C. T. Moore, *New Literary History* 6, No. 1, *On Metaphor* (Autumn, 1974): 5–74 (Published by: The Johns Hopkins University Press).

Drohojowska-Philip, Hunter. *Full Bloom: The Art and Life of Georgia O'Keeffe* (New York: Norton, 2004).

Encarnacao, John. "Musical Structure as Narrative in Rock," *Journal of Multidisciplinary International Studies* 8, No. 1 (January 01, 2011).

Fichte, Johann Gottlieb. *The Science of Knowing: J.G. Fichte's 1804 Lectures on the Wissenschaftslehre* (Albany: State University of New York, 2005).

Flowers of Evil, tr. George Dillon and Edna St. Vincent Millay (New York: Harper and Brothers, 1936).

Fóti, Véronique. "Adversity and Practices of Painting," *Philosophy Today* 60, No. 2 (Spring, 2016): 397–405.

Foucault, Michel. *This Is Not a Pipe*, tr. Harkness (Berkeley: University of California, 1983).

Freud, Sigmund. *Civilization and Its Discontents*, tr. Riviere (New York: Dover, 1944).

Freud, Sigmund. *The Interpretation of Dreams*, tr. Strachey (New York: Basic Books, 2010).

Freud, Sigmund. "The Poet and Daydreaming," in *Collected Papers*, vol. IV (London: Hogarth Press, 1956).

Freud, Sigmund. *Totem and Taboo*, tr. Strachey (New York: Norton, 1950).

Fynsk, Christopher. *Thought and Historicity* (Ithaca: Cornell University Press, 1986).

Gordon, Paul. *Art as the Absolute: Art's Relation to Metaphysics in Kant, Fichte, Schelling, Hegel and Schopenhauer* (New York/London: Bloomsbury Academic, 2015/17).

Gordon, Paul. *Illustration of J. Hillis Miller Word and Image* 22, No. 1 (2006)

Gordon, Paul. *Dial 'M' for Mother* (Madison: Farleigh Dickinson University Press, 2008).

Gordon, Paul. *The Critical Double: Figurative Meaning in Aesthetics* (Tuscaloosa/London: University of Alabama Press, 1995).

Gordon, Paul. *Rapturous Superabundance: Tragedy after Nietzsche* (Chicago: University of Illinois, 2001).

Gorfon, Paul. "Revis(ion)ing Freud's Medusa," *Psychoanalysis, Culture & Society* 19, (March 20, 2014): 113–26.

Griffin, Randall. *Georgia O'Keeffe* (New York: Phaidon, 2014).

Hadot, Pierre. *The Veil of Isis* (Cambridge: Harvard University Press, 2006).

Hegel, Georg Wilhelm Friedrich. *Introductory Lectures on Aesthetics*, tr. Bosanquet (London: Penguin, 1993).

Hegel, Georg Wilhelm Friedrich. *The Phenomenology of Spirit*, tr. Miller (Oxford: Oxford University Press, 1977).

Heidegger, Martin. *Der Satz vom Grund* (Pfullingen: Neske, 1978); *The Principle of Reason*, tr. Lilly (Bloomington: Indiana University Press, 1996).

Heidegger, Martin. *Der Ursprung des Kunstwerkes* (Stuttgart: Reclam, 1960).

Heidegger, Martin. *Introduction to Metaphysic*, tr. Fried/Polt (New Haven: Yale University Press, 2000).

Heidegger, Martin. "The Origin of the Work of Art," in *Poetry, Language, Thought* (New York: Harper and Row, 1971).

Heidegger, Martin. *Sein und Zeit* (Tübingen: Niemeyer, 1993).

Heidegger, Martin. *What is a Thing?* tr. Barton/Deutsch (South Bend: Regnery/Gateway, 1967).

Hoffmann, E. T. A. *Hoffmann's Musical Writings*, ed. Charlton, tr. Clarke (Cambridge: Cambridge University Press, 1989).

Homer. *The Odyssey*, tr. Fitzgerald (New York: Vintage, 1990).

Iser, Wolfgang. *The Act of Reading* (Baltimore: Johns Hopkins University Press, 1978).

Jakobson, Roman. "Two Aspects of Language and Two Types of Aphasic Disturbances," in *On Language* (Cambridge: Harvard University Press, 1995).

James, Henry. "The Figure in the Carpet," in *Eight Tales from the Major Phase* (New York: Norton, 1969).

Joan Michell (ed.), *Ohlsen* (Heidelberg: Kerher Verlag, 2008).

Junod, Phillipe. “The New Paragone,” in *The Arts Entwined: Music and Painting in the Nineteenth Century*, eds. Morton and Schmunk (New York: Garland, 2000).

Kaganovsky, Lilya and Salazkina, Masha (eds.), *Sound, Speech Music in Soviet and Post-Soviet Cinema* (Bloomington: Indiana University Press, 2014).

Kant, Immanuel. “Critique of Teleological Judgment,” in *The Critique of Judgment*, tr. Meredith (Oxford: Clarendon Press, 1952).

Kant, Immanuel. *Preface to Second Edition, Critique of* Pure *Reason*, tr. N. K. Smith (New York: St. Martin’s, 1929).

Kenaan, Hagi. “Tracing Shadows: Reflections on the Origin of Painting,” in *Pictorial Languages and Their Meanings: Liber Amicorum in Honor of Nurith Kenaan-Kedar*, eds. C. Versar and G. Fishof (Tel Aviv: University Publishing, 2006).

Kofman, Sarah. *Nietzsche et la métaphore* (Paris: Galilée, 1985).

Labarthe, Patrick. “Une poétique ambifuë: Les “corresponances,” in *Les Fleurs du mal: Colloque de la Sorbonne* (Paris: Presses de l’Université de Paris-Sorbonne, 2003).

Lissa, Zofia. *Ästhetik der Filmmusik* (Berlin: Henschel, 1965).

Luke, David P. and Terhune, Devin B. “The Induction of Synaesthesia with Chemical Agents: A Systematic Review,” *Frontiers in Psychology* 4 (2013): 753. https://www.ncbi.nlm.nih.gov/pmc/articles/PMC3797969/

Marks, Lawrence E. *The Unity of the Senses: Interrelations Among the Modalities* (New York, San Franscisco, and London: Academic Press, 1978).

Martin, Daria. *Mirror-Touch Synaesthesia: Thresholds of Empathy with Art* (Oxford: Oxford University Press, 2017).

Martin, Daria. “On Colored-Hearing Synaesthesia: Cross-Modal Translations of Sensory Dimensions,” *Psychological Bulletin* 83 (1975): 303–31.

Mathews, Marthiel and Mathews, Jackson. *The Flowers of Evil*, eds. Marthiel and Mathews (New York: New Directions 1989).

Meadows, Patrick. “Baudelaire’s Syncretic Extensions of Synesthesia,” *Symposium* 65, No. 2 (2011): 117–33.

Mervyn, Cooke. *A History of Film Music* (Cambridge: Cambridge University Press, 2008).

Miles, Barry. *Paul McCartney: Many Years From Now* (New York: Henry Holt and Company, 1997).

Miller, J. Hillis. *Illustration* (Cambridge: Harvard University Press, 1992).

Minahen, Charles. “Correspondence Theory and the Case of Baudelaire’s Sphinx Intertext,” *Romance Quarterly* 39, No. 2 (1992).

Morton, Marsha. “From the Other Side,” in *The Arts Entwined: Music and Painting in the Nineteenth Century*, eds. Morton and Schmunk (New York: Garland, 2000).

Nancy, Jean-Luc. *The Birth to Presence* (Stanford: Stanford University Press, 1993).

Nancy, Jean-Luc. *The Ground of the Image* (New York: Fordham, 2005).

Nancy, Jean-Luc. *Listening*, tr. Charlotte Mandell (New York: Fordham University Press, 2002).

Nietzsche, Friedrich. *The Birth of Tragedy*, tr. Gollfing (Garden City: Doubleday, 1956).

Nietzsche, Friedrich. "Truth and Lies in an Extra-Moral Sense," Collected in *Philosophy and Truth*, tr. Breazeale (Atlantic Highlands: Humanities Press, 1979).

Nyerges, Alex Director. "Virginia Museum of Fine Arts, from a review of Robin Lippincott's." *Blue Territory* (Amazon).

Parmiggiani, Sandro. "In Search of a Lost Feeling," in Joan Michell, ed. Ohlsen (Heidelberg: Kerher Verlag, 2008).

Richter, Mario. *Les Fleurs du mal* (Geneva: Slatkine, 2001).

Ricoeur, Paul. *La métaphore vive* (Paris: Seuil, 1975).

Robertson, Robert. *Eisenstein on the Audiovisual: The Montage of Music, Image and Sound in Cinema* (London: Taurus, 2009).

Rouault, Georges. *Mystic Masque: Semblance and Reality in Georges Rouault*, ed. Schlosser (Chicago: University of Chicago Press, 2008).

Schelling, Friedrich Wilhelm Joseph. *System of Transcendental Idealism (1800)*, tr. Heath (Charlottesville: University of Virginia Press, 1978).

Schmidt, Dennis. *Between Word and Image* (Bloomington: Indiana University Press, 2013).

Schneller, Tom. "Modal Interchange and Semantic Resonance in Themes by John Williams: A semiotic examination of contemporary media music," *Journal of Film Music* 6, No. 1 (2013): 49–74.

Schopenhauer, Arthur. *The World as Will and Representation*, vol. 1, tr. Payne (New York: Dover, 1969).

Seraller, Francisco. *Picasso Vollard Suite* (Madrid: NP, 1993).

Shaw-Miller, Simon. *Visible Deeds of Music* (New Haven: Yale, 2002).

Silverman, Kaja. *World Spectators* (Palo Alto: Stanford University Press, 2000).

Simon, Baron-Cohen and Harrison, John E. (eds.), *Synaesthesia* (Oxford: Blackwell Publishers, 1997).

Vallega, Alejandro. "Paul Klee's Originary Painting," *Research in Phenomenology* 43 (2013): 462–74.

Wagner, Geoffrey. *Selected Poems of Charles Baudelaire* (New York: Grove Press, 1974).

Index

www.ingramcontent.com/pod-product-compliance
Lightning Source LLC
Chambersburg PA
CBHW071251180926
51613CB00001B/11
9781501356797